NEW DIRECTIONS FOR CHILD DEVELOPMENT

William Damon, *Brown University*
EDITOR-IN-CHIEF

The Role of Play in the Development of Thought

Marc H. Bornstein
National Institute of Child Health and Human Development

Anne Watson O'Reilly
National Institute of Child Health and Human Development

EDITORS

Number 59, Spring 1993

JOSSEY-BASS PUBLISHERS
San Francisco

THE ROLE OF PLAY IN THE DEVELOPMENT OF THOUGHT
Marc H. Bornstein, Anne Watson O'Reilly (eds.)
New Directions for Child Development, no. 59
William Damon, Editor-in-Chief

Microfilm copies of issues and articles are available in 16mm and 35mm, as well as microfiche in 105mm, through University Microfilms Inc., 300 North Zeeb Road, Ann Arbor, Michigan 48106.

LC 85-644581   ISSN 0195-2269   ISBN 1-55542-688-3

NEW DIRECTIONS FOR CHILD DEVELOPMENT is part of The Jossey-Bass Education Series and is published quarterly by Jossey-Bass Inc., Publishers, 350 Sansome Street, San Francisco, California 94104-1310 (publication number USPS 494-090). Second-class postage paid at San Francisco, California, and at additional mailing offices. POSTMASTER: Send address changes to Jossey-Bass Inc., Publishers, 350 Sansome Street, San Francisco, California 94104-1310.

EDITORIAL CORRESPONDENCE should be sent to the Editor-in-Chief, William Damon, Department of Education, Box 1938, Brown University, Providence, Rhode Island 02912.

Cover photograph by Wernher Krutein/PHOTOVAULT © 1990.

 The paper used in this journal is acid-free and meets the strictest guidelines in the United States for recycled paper (50 percent recycled waste, including 10 percent post-consumer waste). Manufactured in the United States of America.

10% POST CONSUMER WASTE

CONTENTS

EDITORS' NOTES   1
Marc H. Bornstein, Anne Watson O'Reilly

1. Exploratory Play with Objects: Basic Cognitive Processes and   5
Individual Differences
Holly A. Ruff, Lisa M. Saltarelli
Relations between exploratory activity in manipulative play and focused
attention and learning are investigated.

2. Play and Its Relations to Other Mental Functions in the Child   17
Catherine S. Tamis-LeMonda, Marc H. Bornstein
Quantitative and qualitative indexes of child play are examined and related
to other cognitive functions, notably, habituation and language.

3. Pretend Play in High-Risk and Developmentally   29
Delayed Children
Marian Sigman, Rhonda Sena
Uses of pretend play in diagnoses with special populations are presented.

4. Multidimensional Correlates of Individual Variability in   43
Play and Exploration
Theodore D. Wachs
Biological, experiential, and individual differences factors are related to
variation in the nature and amount of children's play and exploration.

5. Caregiver-Child Interaction in Play   55
Anne Watson O'Reilly, Marc H. Bornstein
Social and didactic aspects of caregiver-child interactions are examined with
respect to the development of play and individual variation in children's play
ability.

6. The Development of Play as the Development of Consciousness   67
Loraine McCune
The capacity for consciousness of self and others is posited to arise from
perceptual and representational activities during play.

INDEX   81

EDITORS' NOTES

"Play is children's work." Clichés having to do with the seriousness of children's play abound in our culture. The words *toil* and *toy* share the same Middle English root; indeed, the dictionary's first meaning for *toy* is "tool." Children's play has been likened to practice for later life, and many of our predecessors in the study of play have argued that it is through play that the child learns about the world and how to modify and master the environment. This view of play seems particularly appropriate as a characterization of the activities of children in the very first years of life, as they engage in increasingly sophisticated interactions with objects and people during play. As indicated by the title of this volume, *The Role of Play in the Development of Thought,* the chapters explore one aspect of the seriousness of play.

Theories and definitions of play are historically fertile and contentious grounds. Through their focus on play as the manipulation and examination of the object environment and as an expression of the capacity for symbolic representation, the contributors to this volume converge on an apparently universal aspect of young children's play, namely, its progressive nature. Play appears to be scalable and so provides a situation that merits special attention and exploration from cognitive developmentalists. This volume examines relations between play and the development of other mental abilities in order to further explore this progression, especially with an eye toward using play as an early cognitive assessment tool in both normal and at-risk children. In addition, the correlates of advanced expressions of play in biological, environmental, and social interaction are discussed, and the use of symbolic play as an index of the child's developing consciousness of self and others is presented.

In Chapter One, Holly A. Ruff and Lisa M. Saltarelli examine individual variation in infants' exploratory play with objects, and they delve into basic cognitive processes that may be deduced from infant play. They separate manipulative play into exploratory and nonexploratory types and find that only exploratory play relates to focused attention and learning. Their research indicates that infants are more resistant to distraction during exploratory play, show declines in exploratory behavior as objects of play become more familiar, and explore more when presented with novel objects. Their work also emphasizes the importance of considering context in understanding the processes entailed in exploratory behaviors. This chapter concludes with a discussion of relations between exploratory play and mastery motivation, highlighting the use of play in research on both cognitive and motivational development.

In Chapter Two, Catherine S. Tamis-LeMonda and Marc H. Bornstein review their work on quantitative and qualitative indexes of play, developmental interrelations between the two, and relations of each to other cognitive abilities in children, most notably language. They find consistent relations between duration and level in play across various time periods in early development, and they find that developments in play and language parallel one another. In addition, their research indicates that measures of spontaneous activity and habituation in infancy predict play at later ages as well as a latent construct of language and play.

In Chapter Three, Marian Sigman and Rhonda Sena discuss the use of pretend play as a cognitive assessment tool. They report on the developmental progression—or failure of progression—of play in a diverse set of at-risk populations: preterm, drug-exposed, malnourished, Down syndrome, mentally retarded, and autistic children. They examine the relative standing of play in these different groups as well as associations between play and language in each group, focusing particularly on the growing body of research on play in autistic children. For Sigman and Sena, play serves a role in the early identification of cognitive disorders and is a means toward understanding and differentiating those disorders.

In Chapter Four, Theodore D. Wachs discusses the many and varied correlates of play, focusing on environmental, biological, and individual differences factors. He argues that one way to explore links between play and thought is to search for common determinants of each, and he emphasizes consideration of the determinants of play and thought in combination, not isolation. Wachs brings to bear on his insights about play very provocative cross-cultural work from Egypt. His studies explore multiple correlates of morbidity, nutrition, and the caregiving environment on toddlers' play sophistication in a non-Western culture, thereby also addressing the universality of play. He concludes with a speculative, yet appealing, discussion of variability in individual characteristics of child play in interaction with variability in parental characteristics, suggesting that play may be a function of the "goodness of fit" between child and caregiver styles.

In Chapter Five, we return to the issue of environmental correlates of play, exploring variation in child play from solitary play to play in the social context of mother-child interaction. We discuss two dimensions of caregiver behaviors, social and didactic, in the domain of play, looking at caregiver behaviors during child play, at changes in these behaviors as the child develops, and at relations of individual differences in these behaviors to individual differences in child play. Caregivers show sensitivity to child ability levels in play, and there is strong evidence that children are attentive and responsive to parental activities in play. This chapter stresses the extent and limits of current research on caregiver-child interactions in play, as it lays the groundwork for future explorations of the impact of parental behaviors on mental growth in the realm of child play.

Finally, in Chapter Six, Loraine McCune analyzes higher-order levels of play in a discussion of play as the development of consciousness. McCune argues that the capacity for consciousness of self and others (a "theory of mind") arises from developing representational as well as perceptual activities, in particular representational and perceptual activities during play. Her premise is that the ability to direct attention intentionally to internal representations as well as external perceptions is the hallmark of consciousness, and she looks for evidence of such ability in the developmental sequence of symbolic play in young children. Her chapter emphasizes the interaction of social and cognitive features of play in creating a differentiated representation of self and others in relation to the object world.

Together, these chapters explore the dual quantitative and qualitative nature of play, determinants of play development from inside as well as outside the young child, symbolic and highly intellectual aspects of play, and play across diverse contexts. In addition, the intimate connection between the child as a social being, developing within the context of social interactions, and representational play is highlighted. In all, the crucial role of play in children's developing cognition is emphasized.

Children's play holds perennial fascination for adults; we count ourselves among them. All of us, at one time or another, have paused in what we were doing to observe and reflect on a child at play and to see in that play the child's mental ability and functioning. This volume takes a small step toward formalizing and, more important, sharing those observations.

Marc H. Bornstein
Anne Watson O'Reilly
Editors

MARC H. BORNSTEIN is senior research scientist and head of Child and Family Research at the National Institute of Child Health and Human Development, Bethesda, Maryland. His interests include experimental, methodological, comparative, developmental, cross-cultural, and aesthetic psychology.

ANNE WATSON O'REILLY is postdoctoral fellow in Child and Family Research at the National Institute of Child Health and Human Development. Her interests include early cognitive development and language acquisition.

Manipulative play can be decomposed into exploratory and nonexploratory activity; only exploration is linked to focused attention and learning.

Exploratory Play with Objects: Basic Cognitive Processes and Individual Differences

Holly A. Ruff, Lisa M. Saltarelli

From five to twelve months of age, infants' manipulative skills expand and become more integrated. When faced with a graspable novel object, infants may respond in a variety of ways. They will almost certainly reach, grasp, and look at the object; they may then mouth it, finger it, bang it, push it around, show it to the mother, and drop or throw it. Given the amount of time devoted to such manipulative play, it seems reasonable to suppose that this play is important in infants' learning about the inanimate world and their own efficacy in that world. On the other hand, manipulative play involves a stream of activity with rapid shifts from one act to another. We may not do justice to the complexity of the underlying processes if we assume that all manipulative activity has only one function (Ruff, 1989).

Exploratory Versus Nonexploratory Activity

When, in the course of manipulative activity with an object, is an infant actually focused on, exploring, and learning about the object per se? We suggest that exploratory activity can be separated from nonexploratory activity and that only during the former is the infant's attention engaged for the purpose of gathering information about the object, its properties, and its functions. Certain activities may be inherently exploratory. Some activities may be exploratory at some times and not at others; when they are not exploratory, they may function to soothe the infant, raise the infant's arousal level, give the infant a break from more effortful activity, or simply serve to maintain contact with the object while the infant attends to something else.

The major exploratory activity with which we have worked is examining. First described by Užgiris (1967) as a schema, it involves looking at the object while simultaneously fingering it, turning it around, and transferring it from hand to hand. In our coding system, we have added a requirement that these activities be accompanied by a serious, intent facial expression. We also include other deliberate activity under the rubric of examining, for example, an infant's slow banging of an object against a high-chair tray while looking at it with knit brows. Most often, however, activity such as banging occurs in a rapid, stereotyped way, sometimes with the infant grinning and looking elsewhere. Such activity is excluded because the infant does not appear to be attending to the object as such or to be very attentive at all (see Ruff and Lawson, 1990, for further details).

Experimental evidence (Ruff, 1984; Ruff and Dubiner, 1987) confirms this general distinction between examining and more vigorous, nonexploratory play. In a recent study, however, we also separated mouthing of the objects into exploratory and nonexploratory subtypes (Ruff, Saltarelli, Capozzoli, and Dubiner, 1992). We define exploratory mouthing as mouthing that is followed immediately by a look at the object. When such looks are observed, it seems as though the infant is confirming visually something interesting that was picked up by the mouthing that came before. The immediacy of the look also suggests that the infant's attention is focused on the object per se. Any time the infant removes the object from the mouth and looks elsewhere, the preceding episode of mouthing is considered to be nonexploratory.

Learning During Exploratory Activity

If our definitions are valid, then exploratory activity should be related to learning whereas other activity in the same session should not be. To test this hypothesis, we used habituation and recovery as indexes of learning. Habituation refers to the decrement in attention or responsiveness that often occurs with repetition of a particular event; recovery refers to the increase in responsiveness that occurs when a novel event follows the repeated, now familiar, event. Our hypothesis was that if an activity is exploratory, it should relate systematically to the novelty of objects, declining with continued experience with an object, and increasing when a novel object is presented.

In a cross-sectional study of five- to eleven-month-old infants (Ruff, Saltarelli, Capozzoli, and Dubiner, 1992), we presented the children with a series of novel objects, one at a time, for three-minute familiarization periods. After the first period of play, the object was removed and presented again for a one-and-one-half-minute trial. Then the next object was presented. This cycle was repeated four times. Our expectation was that the duration of exploratory activity—examining and mouthing with immediate looks afterward—would decline from the first half of the familiarization trial to the second half and decline again or stay the same with the re-presentation of the same object. The presentation of the novel object, however, would lead to an increase or recovery. In contrast, we expected that there would be no systematic relation between novelty and the duration of other types of visual and manipulative activity or other types of mouthing.

Our expectations were confirmed statistically. Examining declined significantly over the course of the familiarization trial. It never recovered when the same object was re-presented but showed a strong and significant recovery whenever a novel object was presented. Other looking and manipulating showed no systematic pattern of change within or across trials. The same contrast was found for mouthing with looks afterward versus mouthing without such looks. Further analyses showed that the results for mouthing with looks afterward were not simply a function of either the frequency or the duration of looking. Thus, the data supported our contention that some mouthing is indeed used for gathering information about the object and that other types of mouthing serve other functions (see Ruff, Saltarelli, Capozzoli, and Dubiner, 1992, for further details).

The overall pattern of results suggests that the activities we define here as exploratory, in contrast to nonexploratory activities, are linked to learning. This is so, we think, because exploratory activities involve an engagement of focused attention whereas the nonexploratory activities do not.

Exploratory Activity and Focused Attention

The term *focused attention* implies both greater selectivity and greater intensity than does more casual attention. During focused attention, an individual is likely to be responsive to a narrower range of input, to show decreased variability in physical activity, and to be less relaxed than during casual attention. Attention is not only actively directed to a particular object but also actively inhibited from other objects. Focused attention is effortful, and it is important when there is something to be learned or accomplished. In the context of infants' manipulative play, it would seem most adaptive for infants to be focused when they are faced with something new (Ruff, 1986b) or are trying to master a particular aspect of an object's function (Jennings, 1991). Otherwise, it is adaptive to be somewhat more relaxed and unselective in order to monitor the environment.

Resistance to Distraction During Focused Attention

One aspect of attention that is not evident from summary statistics is the ebb and flow that occurs. Schachtel (1954, p. 310) wrote that "each focal act [of attention], as a rule, consists of not just *one* sustained approach to the object . . . but of *several renewed* approaches. They . . . usually—probably always —alternate or oscillate between a more passive, receptive, reactive phase and a more active, taking-hold, structuring, integrating phase." If episodes of exploratory activity are also periods of focused attention, as we hypothesize, then infants should be less distractible when they are exploring than when they are engaged in other kinds of activity. To test this possibility, we (Saltarelli, Capozzoli, and Ruff, 1990) presented eight- and ten-month-old infants with novel objects. During their play with these objects, slides appeared on a rearview projector that stood off to the child's right and required approximately a ninety-degree turn of the head to see (Anderson, Choi, and Lorch, 1987). The advancing of the slide was accompanied by an audible sound, making the distractor both auditory and visual. We counted on the infant's great interest in manipulating toys to make the objects somewhat more potent than the slides, but we also wanted the slides to be salient enough to be somewhat distracting. These conditions were met.

The specific question was whether the infants would be less distractible when they were engaged in exploration at the time that a slide appeared than if they were engaged in nonexploratory activity at the time. We combined examining and mouthing with looks afterward into a single category of exploratory activity. We then combined other looking and manipulating and other mouthing into a single category of nonexploratory activity. In this sense, we had two conditions defined by the activity at the time of the slide presentation. To address the question of whether there were different degrees of distractibility in these different conditions, we used two measures of distractibility (Anderson, Choi, and Lorch, 1987). The first was the percentage of opportunities per condition in which the infant actually turned and looked at the slide. The second was the time it took to turn and face the projector on those occasions when the infant actually made a head turn.

We found that the ten-month-olds, but not the eight-month-olds, were less likely to turn their heads when they were exploring the object at the time that the slide came on than when they were not exploring. Thus, only the data from the older infants were in the direction of the hypothesis (42 percent during exploration, 51 percent during nonexploratory activity, $p = .03$). Infants at both ages, however, took longer to turn their heads if the onset of the slide occurred during exploratory activity than if it occurred during nonexploratory activity (1.8 versus 1.6 seconds, respectively, $p = .03$). This result argues for an inhibitory influence during focused attention that slows down the response to competing stimulation.

The discrepancy between the eight-month-olds and the ten-month-olds in the probability of turning their heads is interesting. During exploratory activity, the two age groups did not differ (43 percent versus 42 percent, respectively); however, the eight-month-olds were significantly less likely to turn during nonexploratory activity (37 percent versus 51 percent, respectively). We think that this is a function of the greater amount of banging in which the eight-month-olds engaged. Because the sound of the slide being advanced signified that there was something potentially interesting to look at, an infant may not have been distracted if the sound were masked by the sound of the object hitting the table. To test the plausibility of this interpretation, we divided the entire sample in half, regardless of age, according to the duration of banging. Of the children who were below the median in banging, thirteen out of eighteen (72 percent) responded in the hypothesized direction. Only 39 percent of the children who were above the median in banging showed the hypothesized pattern.

If resistance to distraction is higher during exploratory play, then such play may well be somewhat more effortful in a cognitive sense. According to one model (Kahneman, 1973), effort is defined as the extent to which the subject's limited capacity is being used; thus, infants are less likely to be distracted during exploration because they have fewer resources available for attention to other events in the environment. Another possibility, however, is that effort is defined in part by the degree to which competing responses are inhibited; in this case, infants are less likely to be distracted and are likely to turn more slowly when they are distracted from focused attention because inhibitory processes are more active than they are during casual attention. In any case, the data from this study generally support our contention that infants' attention is more focused on objects during exploratory play than during other types of play with objects.

Relations of Exploratory Activity to Other Measures of Attention

The data from yet another of our studies offer further validation of the distinction between exploratory and nonexploratory play and also confirm the link between exploratory play and attention. In this study, seven- and nine-month-olds were observed in three different conditions. One condition was very much like the previous two studies, where the infants were presented with single objects for periods of manipulative play. The second condition involved the presentation of a puppet for a series of six ten-second trials, and the third was a period of play on the floor with a small bucket of toys. The infants sat on their mothers' laps for the first two procedures; during floor play, the mothers were filling out questionnaires, and the infants were more on their own. The questionnaire was the Rothbart Infant Behavior Questionnaire (Rothbart, 1981).

From both manipulative play with single objects and floor play, we obtained the duration of exploratory and nonexploratory play. In the puppet procedure, we measured the duration of looking at the puppet. The goal of the data analysis was to examine the relations of exploratory and nonexploratory play with single objects to attention in the other two conditions and to the mother's judgment of her infant's general attentiveness (duration of orienting in Rothbart, 1991). Our expectation was that only exploratory activity would be related to the mother's rating of attention.

Exploratory play with single objects was related to exploratory activity with the toys during floor play ($r = .44$, $p < .05$), but less so to other looking at the toys. Nonexploratory play was not related to either. It is noteworthy that, although duration of exploratory play was not related to duration of looking at the puppets, nonexploratory play was unexpectedly and positively related to it ($r = .40$, $p < .05$).

When all of these measures were compared to the mothers' ratings of attention, the resulting correlations were consistent with our expectations. Mothers' judgments of their infants' attention on the measure of duration of orienting were related positively to exploratory play during both single-object manipulation ($r = .30$, $p < .10$) and floor play ($r = .44$, $p < .05$) but negatively related to nonexploratory play with single objects ($r = -.31, p < .10$). This last correlation is significantly different from the other two. Duration of orienting was negatively related to looking at the puppet ($r = -.26$).

The data therefore support the view that exploratory play involves more focused sustained attention than does nonexploratory play. An intriguing aspect of the data is that the mothers' ratings of attention are negatively related to both nonexploratory play with objects and looking at the puppets, and that the latter two variables are positively related to each other. This pattern of results suggests that looking at an event may involve a somewhat different kind of attention than characterizes more active exploration and play with toys.

Effect of Context on Duration of Attention

Research by Bornstein and Colombo and their colleagues (for example, Bornstein and Sigman, 1986; Colombo and Mitchell, 1990) has suggested that duration of looking is negatively related to better functioning in terms of novelty preferences, language development, and later performance on cognitive tests. Studies of looking in high-risk infants have led to the same conclusion (Cohen and Parmelee, 1983). The interpretation of all of these findings is that the duration of looking reflects the speed and efficiency with which information is acquired.

In the context of play with toys, however, longer durations of more focused attention are characteristic of normal infants when compared to high-risk infants (Ruff, 1986a) and are predictors of better cognitive functioning at later ages (Ruff, 1988). Similar findings with regard to concurrent relations have been found by Tamis-LeMonda and Bornstein (1990; this volume). Our comparison of conditions in the study of seven- and nine-month-olds emphasizes this contrast because the results differ according to whether attention is defined as looking at, but not interacting with, external events or as exploration of objects in conditions that allow a greater range of activity.

This potential discrepancy led us to examine others' research on changes with age in the total duration of looking in three different contexts. In the first context—repeated presentations of the same event for the infant to look at—there was a consistent decline with age in the amount of time that the infants devoted to looking at those events (Bornstein, Pêcheux, and Lécuyer, 1988; Colombo and Mitchell, 1990; Lewis, Goldberg, and Campbell, 1969). In order to make comparisons of this decline across contexts more direct, we present data here from fixed-trial procedures, where the measure of duration was the percentage of available time spent in looking. Figure 1.1 shows the data from two studies by Lewis, Goldberg, and Campbell (1969). The top line represents the average of data from three cross-sectional studies of three- to thirteen-month-olds, where there were four to nine thirty-second trials in which the repeated stimulus was a flashing light. The other line is from a study in which there were nine trials with a colored slide of curved-line segments. In contrast, Figure 1.2 shows what happens to looking with age when the infant is presented with single objects for manipulative play. The bottom line depicts the results of the study of five- to eleven-month-olds already described. The top line depicts the results of a study of six-, nine-, and twelve-month-olds given quite different objects (Ruff, 1986b). In neither case was there a systematic change with age. Finally, Figure 1.3 illustrates changes occurring in the

**Figure 1.1. Looking During
Repeated Presentation of Same Event**

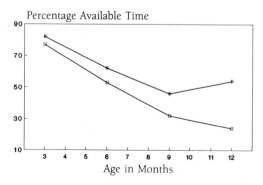

Source: Based on Lewis, Goldberg, and Campbell, 1969.

Figure 1.2. Looking During Manipulative Play with Single Objects

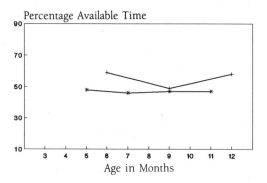

Source: Based on Ruff, 1986b.

Figure 1.3. Looking During Free Play with Multiple Objects

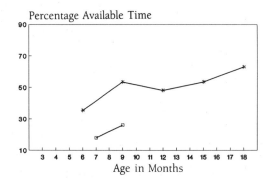

Sources: Based on Lauren Adamson, personal communication, April 6, 1992; Bakeman and Adamson, 1984.

context of free play with multiple objects. The bottom line reflects the change from seven to nine months in the study previously described here; the top line reflects the results of a larger study by Adamson and Bakeman (Lauren Adamson, personal communication, April 6, 1992; Bakeman and Adamson, 1984). In both cases, duration of looking increases with age. Thus, we are confronted with three different situations and three different patterns of change in looking over different age groups.

These comparisons suggest that context is an essential consideration in understanding the processes underlying a behavior such as looking. It may be that the decline of looking with age in the habituation paradigm reflects increased efficiency and speed, but only when a relatively simple target is repeatedly presented. Once an infant can manipulate objects, the situation becomes richer in information and visual attention may be enhanced or guided by the information that the infant picks up haptically and aurally. Older infants, though they may learn faster, may explore more facets of the object, resulting in a similar level of looking across ages. When the infant is presented with an array of toys in unconstrained circumstances, the possibilities are even greater. The increase in looking with age may reflect the infant's enhanced capacity to both explore and exploit object properties and to attend to relations among objects.

Variation in developmental patterns of looking across contexts suggests further that looking can reflect the operation of several underlying processes. We think that the differentiation of attention during play into focused and more casual attention can inform us about these processes. Although, with manipulation of single objects, there is virtually no change in total looking with age, a steady and significant increase is seen over age in focused attention as manifested in examining as opposed to other looking and manipulating (Ruff, Saltarelli, Capozzoli, Dubiner, 1992). In the free-play context where we observed an increase in looking from seven to nine months, only examining increased; other looking and manipulating showed no change. If the same kind of distinction could be made in the habituation paradigm (see Bornstein, 1985), it would further refine our understanding of the nature of developmental changes in attention.

Individual Differences

Although we have illustrated these points within the framework of developmental changes, we began with the individual differences that are implied in the negative correlation between looking at events and interacting with objects. It may be that children who are competent to act on objects are less content to observe events passively. Shorter looking and longer active exploration would thus be related concurrently. Predictively, it may be that infants who learn quickly and look less at pictures and events in the early part of infancy may later see more possibilities in an object during manipulative play. A third possibility is that children who show shorter durations of looking in the first six or seven months, yet later explore and play for longer periods, are more flexible in their deployment of attention. We know that the ability to disengage attention develops during the first year (Johnson, Posner, and Rothbart, 1991); older, and presumably more mature, infants readily disengage visual attention unless there is something complex and changing to hold their interest. Individual infants may also vary in the readiness with which they disengage and shift attention (Rothbart and Derryberry, 1981).

As was the case for developmental trends, an understanding of underlying processes is important for the treatment of individual differences in attention. The distinction between focused and casual attention in the observation of infants may help us to distinguish between short lookers who are fast learners and short lookers who fail to be aroused enough by the event to attend to it. On the other hand, the same distinction may help us to differentiate long lookers who are actively exploring many aspects of the events and objects that they encounter from long lookers who are merely perseverating.

Conclusion

Active exploration of objects in play is one way that infants provide themselves with changing stimulation and information; during their activity, focused attention is engaged and reengaged. Focused attention in play with objects is initiated and sustained, in part, by a motivation to learn about and master the environment. This is one of the assumptions underlying the work on mastery motivation; Jennings (1991, p. 3) observes that "more motivated children spontaneously exert more effort and focused attention when interacting with objects and thus use their most sophisticated levels more often." In discussing the development of focal attention, Schachtel (1954, p. 312) notes that "attention to . . . small objects is another important step—a change from attending only reactively to what impinges, to attending actively to an object which arouses curiosity and interest." Individual infants may vary in the extent to which they can bring the different facets of an object into focus; the ability to do so depends on knowledge and on manipulatory skills. Thus, the observation of focused exploratory play in infants provides us with a base for studying both cognitive and motivational development as well as the rich and fascinating variation among individuals.

References

Anderson, D. R., Choi, H. P., and Lorch, E. P. "Attentional Inertia Reduces Distractibility During Young Children's TV Viewing." *Child Development,* 1987, *58,* 798–806.

Bakeman, R., and Adamson, L. B. "Coordinating Attention to People and Objects in Mother-Infant and Peer-Infant Interaction." *Child Development,* 1984, *55,* 1278–1289.

Bornstein, M. H. "Habituation of Attention as a Measure of Visual Information Processing in Human Infants: Summary, Systematization, and Synthesis." In G. Gottlieb and N. A. Krasnegor (eds.), *Development of Audition and Vision During the First Year of Postnatal Life: A Methodological Overview.* Norwood, N.J.: Ablex, 1985.

Bornstein, M. H., Pêcheux, M.-G., and Lécuyer, R. "Visual Habituation in Infants: Development and Rearing Circumstances." *Psychological Research,* 1988, *50,* 130–133.

Bornstein, M. H., and Sigman, M. D. "Continuity in Mental Development from Infancy." *Child Development,* 1986, *57,* 251–274.

Cohen, S. E., and Parmelee, A. H. "Prediction of Five-Year Stanford-Binet Scores in Preterm Infants." *Child Development,* 1983, *54,* 1242–1253.

Colombo, J., and Mitchell, D. W. "Individual Differences in Early Visual Attention: Fixation Time and Information Processing." In J. Colombo and J. W. Fagen (eds.), *Individual Differences in Infancy: Reliability, Stability, and Prediction*. Hillsdale, N.J.: Erlbaum, 1990.

Jennings, K. D. "Early Development of Mastery Motivation and Its Relation to the Self-Concept." In M. Bullock (ed.), *The Development of Intentional Action: Cognitive, Motivational, and Interactive Processes*. Basel, Switzerland: Karger, 1991.

Johnson, M. H., Posner, M. I., and Rothbart, M. K. "Components of Visual Orienting in Early Infancy: Contingency Learning, Anticipatory Looking, and Disengaging." *Journal of Cognitive Neuroscience*, 1991, *3*, 335–344.

Kahneman, D. *Attention and Effort*. Englewood Cliffs, N.J.: Prentice Hall, 1973.

Lewis, M., Goldberg, S., and Campbell, H. *A Developmental Study of Information Processing Within the First Years of Life: Response Decrement to a Redundant Signal*. Monographs of the Society for Research in Child Development, vol. 34 (serial no. 9). Chicago: University of Chicago Press, 1969.

Rothbart, M. K. "Measurement of Temperament in Infancy." *Child Development*, 1981, *52*, 569–578.

Rothbart, M. K., and Derryberry, D. "Development of Individual Differences in Temperament." In M. E. Lamb and A. L. Brown (eds.), *Advances in Developmental Psychology*. Vol. 1. Hillsdale, N.J.: Erlbaum, 1981.

Ruff, H. A. "Infants' Manipulative Exploration of Objects: Effects of Age and Object Characteristics." *Developmental Psychology*, 1984, *20*, 9–20.

Ruff, H. A. "Attention and Organization of Behavior in High-Risk Infants." *Journal of Developmental and Behavioral Pediatrics*, 1986a, *7*, 298–301.

Ruff, H. A. "Components of Attention During Infants' Manipulative Exploration." *Child Development*, 1986b, *57*, 105–114.

Ruff, H. A. "The Measurement of Attention in High-Risk Infants." In P. M. Vietze and H. G. Vaughan (eds.), *Early Identification of Infants with Developmental Disabilities*. Philadelphia: Grune & Stratton, 1988.

Ruff, H. A. "The Infants' Use of Visual and Haptic Information in the Recognition of Objects." *Canadian Journal of Psychology*, 1989, *43*, 302–319.

Ruff, H. A., and Dubiner, K. "Stability of Individual Differences in Infants' Manipulation and Exploration of Objects." *Perceptual and Motor Skills*, 1987, *64*, 1095–1101.

Ruff, H. A., and Lawson, K. R. "Development of Sustained, Focused Attention in Young Children During Free Play." *Developmental Psychology*, 1990, *26*, 85–93.

Ruff, H. A., Saltarelli, L. M., Capozzoli, M., and Dubiner, K. "The Differentiation of Activity in Infants' Exploration of Objects." *Developmental Psychology*, 1992, *28*, 851–861.

Saltarelli, L. M., Capozzoli, M., and Ruff, H. A. "Focused Attention and Distractibility." Paper presented at the biennial meeting of the International Conference on Infant Studies, Montreal, Quebec, Canada, April 1990.

Schachtel, E. G. "The Development of Focal Attention and the Emergence of Reality." *Psychiatry*, 1954, *17*, 309–324.

Tamis-LeMonda, C. S., and Bornstein, M. H. "Language, Play, and Attention at One Year." *Infant Behavior and Development*, 1990, *13*, 85–98.

Uzgiris, I. C. "Ordinality in the Development of Schemas for Relating to Objects." In J. Hellmuth (ed.), *Exceptional Infant*. Vol. 1: *The Normal Infant*. Seattle: Special Child, 1967.

HOLLY A. RUFF *is professor of pediatrics and director of the Division of Behavioral Sciences at the Albert Einstein College of Medicine, Yeshiva University, New York City. Her research is conducted at the Rose F. Kennedy Center for Research in Mental Retardation and Human Development and has been funded by grants from the National Institute of Child Health and Human Development, National Institute of Mental Health, and National Science Foundation.*

LISA M. SALTARELLI *was postdoctoral fellow at the Albert Einstein College of Medicine and is currently research associate at the Center for the Study of Learning and Attention Disorders at Yale University, New Haven, Connecticut.*

Two indexes of toddler play, duration of attention and level of sophistication, are shown to interrelate, to predict one another over time, and to be predicted by infant activity and habituation as well as by aspects of toddlers' own emerging language abilities.

Play and Its Relations to Other Mental Functions in the Child

Catherine S. Tamis-LeMonda, Marc H. Bornstein

Researchers and theoreticians have often speculated about the nature and correlates of children's early play. What is play like? How does play change over the course of childhood? What inner abilities might play reflect?

Our investigations concern one specific form of play, children's operations on objects, in a circumscribed period of development, the first two years of life. Our research focuses on play development during this period because of the dramatic changes that occur in the sophistication and goal-directedness of children's object actions. Specifically, play over the first two years is characterized by impressive developmental achievements of symbolic activity and enhanced abilities to sustain and regulate attention. In parallel with these changes in play, children demonstrate marked spurts in receptive and productive language (Bates, O'Connell, and Shore, 1987; Belsky, Goode, and Most, 1980; Fein, 1981; McCune-Nicolich, 1981). The parallels in development between play and language have suggested to many that individual differences in play might index underlying representational abilities in children (Bates, Bretherton, Shore, and McNew, 1983; Bornstein, Vibbert, Tal, and O'Donnell, 1992; Fein, 1981; McCune-Nicolich, 1981; Piaget, 1962; Rubin, Fein, and Vandenberg, 1983; Tamis-LeMonda

Catherine S. Tamis-LeMonda was supported by research grants HD20559 and HD20807, and Marc H. Bornstein was supported by research grants HD20559 and HD20807 and by a Research Career Development Award HD00521, from the National Institute of Child Health and Human Development. We thank L. Cyphers, K. Dine, G. Fitzmaurice, J. Hampson, R. Kahana-Kalman, A. Melstein-Damast, K. Nelson, A. O'Reilly, J. Tanaka, B. Wright, and M. Zamor for comments and assistance.

and Bornstein, 1989, 1990, 1991; Vibbert and Bornstein, 1989). Here we focus on two salient indexes of play—duration of attention and level of sophistication—and we ask how these indexes of play relate to one another and to other measures of mental functioning in the young child.

Two Indexes of Play

It is possible to characterize play activities in several ways. *Quantitative* measures of play, such as frequency and duration, consider how much activity is exhibited by the child and for how long. *Qualitative* measures of play focus on the content or nature of play actions, for example, by classifying play according to level of sophistication (McCune-Nicolich, 1981) or thematic content (Dixon and Shore, in press). Here we include quantitative and qualitative assessments of children's object actions by considering two core indexes of children's play, *duration* and *level*. Duration of attention measures the time that children spend engaged with an object. Level of play sophistication is typically based on Guttman scalings of particular play actions across development (see Belsky and Most, 1981). Our use of the term *sophistication* is based on the progressive nature of play, especially the increasing degree of symbolic activity or pretense that characterizes play.[1]

Duration and level are conceptually distinct measures of play: Children can play at lower or higher levels for shorter or longer durations. Thus, a child could engage in repeated mouthing and examining of an object (a relatively elementary level activity) for prolonged temporal stretches, or a child could "make a doll wave" (vicarious pretense) and immediately set the doll aside upon terminating the act. One is operating at a relatively lower level of play sophistication, but doing so in a sustained manner; the other engaging in a high level of play that lasts only momentarily. However, duration and level of play could also be coordinated. Thus, a child might engage in relatively short attention bouts at lower levels of play, or engage in more sophisticated play for longer durations. In practice, quantitative and qualitative measures of play are often linked; individual differences in children in duration of attention are typically associated with individual differences in level of sophistication.

The studies that we report here address the following questions concerning these two indexes of play, their interrelations, and their relations to other mental functions in the child. First, how do duration and level of play change between infancy and the second year of life? To date, few researchers have included both indexes when characterizing children's play. Assessments of play that consider attention and sophistication together can provide a more comprehensive picture of the changing nature of children's early exploration. Second, how do measures of duration and level in play relate to one another at various ages over early development?

Third, how do each of the two indexes of play relate to other mental abilities in the child? By investigating associations between the twin measures of play, as well as between play and other aspects of childhood cognition, we can illuminate models of early mental functioning. For example, covariation between duration and level in play might suggest that a child's overt actions tap a common underlying component of ability in the child, or, alternatively, that the two are functionally codependent. Distinct associations between different indexes of play and other aspects of early cognition would suggest that play is conceptually and empirically modular. In a broader perspective, a componential model of early play implicates multidimensionality of mind.

Finally, this chapter explores the infant antecedents of variation among toddlers in duration and level in play. In investigating the origins of toddlers' play, we sought to identify potential stabilities across periods of substantive developmental transition. Two predictors were considered: infants' spontaneous activity at home and laboratory habituation. These measures are thought to reflect processes similar to those tapped by later indexes of play duration and level—specifically, attention and cognitive sophistication (Bornstein and Sigman, 1986).

Studying Child Play and Language

Our studies are based on home and laboratory assessments of children and their mothers. Families were recruited from private pediatric groups in New York City and are from middle-class households in which the majority of mothers have completed four years of college. We have seen several cohorts of children, with sample sizes ranging between twenty and fifty children.

Across samples, children were observed at home at five, nine, thirteen, seventeen, and twenty-one months of age. In one cohort, toddler play data were based on fifteen minutes of free play with mothers. In a second longitudinal cohort, play data were based on ten minutes of solitary child play at the various ages. In both alone play and interactive play settings, children were seated on the floor with a set of toys, including a clown doll, book, ball, blocks, nesting set, teapot and cover, cups and saucers, spoons, toy telephone, and toy vehicle. During interactive play, mothers were asked to remain seated with their children and to do whatever was typical for them during their toddlers' play. The assessment of children's play in the different settings (that is, with and without mother) permitted comparison of predictive patterns across methodologies and samples. As our focus was on child play and associations between play and other mental functions in the child, over and above maternal contributions, assessments of toddler play during collaborative interactions covaried mothers' play from toddler performance.

In one cohort, at five months an infant-control habituation paradigm was administered in the laboratory, and a measure of peak looking time was obtained. Within one week of this laboratory assessment, mothers and infants were observed in their homes during one hour of naturalistic interaction, and a composite measure of the sampled frequency of infants' vocalization, touching of objects, or visual exploration of their environment and a composite measure of the sampled frequency of mothers' didactic stimulation (that is, how much mothers encouraged their infants to attend to the environment) were obtained (Bornstein and Tamis-LeMonda, 1990). In addition, sustained attention (equal to the longest attention bout) was calculated for examining (looking and manipulating) and for producing effects (for example, banging blocks).

Duration and Level in Play. To obtain data on duration of play at nine to twenty-one months, each child's orientation during play was divided into attention episodes. An attention episode was defined as visual orientation to a target play object lasting a minimum of two seconds. The offset of an episode was signaled when the infant turned away from the target toy for more than two seconds. For each child, total time attending as well as the average duration of the two longest episodes of uninterrupted attention—sustained overall attention—were calculated.

To obtain data on level of play, the frequencies of eight play levels were coded: (1) unitary functional activity, (2) inappropriate combinatorial

Table 2.1. Toddler Play Levels

Play Level	Definition
Nonsymbolic	
1. Unitary functional	Production of an effect that is unique to a single object
2. Inappropriate combinatorial	Inappropriate juxtaposition of two or more objects
3. Appropriate combinatorial	Appropriate juxtaposition of two or more objects
4. Transitional play	Approximation of pretense but without confirmatory evidence
Symbolic	
5. Self-directed pretense	Clear pretense activity directed toward self
6. Other-directed pretense	Clear pretense activity directed toward other
7. Sequential pretense	Linking of two or more pretense actions
8. Substitution pretense	Pretense activity involving one or more object substitutions

activity, (3) appropriate combinatorial activity, (4) transitional play, (5) self-directed pretense, (6) other-directed pretense, (7) sequential pretense, and (8) substitutional pretense (see Table 2.1). A level value for nonsymbolic play was computed by summing totals for play levels 1 through 4. These nonsymbolic play actions are consistent with categories of simple manipulation and relational play used by Sigman and Sena (this volume) and by Wachs (this volume). A level value for symbolic play was computed by summing totals for play levels 5 through 8. This symbolic play category is similar to the symbolic category defined by McCune (this volume) and to the functional and symbolic categories defined by Sigman and Sena (this volume) and by Wachs (this volume).

Child Language. Mothers were probed about their children's receptive and productive vocabularies at various ages, starting from nine months and continuing through twenty-one months. Interviews were based on modified versions of the Bates, Bretherton, and Snyder (1988) inventory and the MacArthur Communicative Development Inventories (Fenson and others, 1991). Interviews at the younger ages emphasized language comprehension, and those at older ages emphasized language production. Data obtained from the interviews included total number of words understood or produced at monthly intervals.

At twenty-one months, data from language interviews were augmented with observational measures of toddlers' production from the videotaped segments. (At younger ages, toddlers rarely spoke intelligible words; in instances when they did, they did not link morphemes.) Measures included assessments of grammar (mean length of utterance [MLU] calculated as the average length in morphemes of toddlers' five longest utterances) and semantic diversity (the number of different semantic categories that children express in their speech, for example, actor, action, possession).

Maternal Play, Language, and IQ. We coded mothers' demonstrations and solicitations of symbolic play based on the eight-level play scale developed for toddlers. In addition, frequency of mothers' referential statements during collaborative play was tabulated. In analyses that assessed toddler play in relation to toddler language, mothers' referential statements were covaried from toddlers' language, and mothers' play was covaried from toddlers' play. This enabled us to examine links among aspects of mental functioning in children independently of their mothers' contributions.

How Do the Two Indexes of Play Change Over Early Development?

We first examined changes in the total time that children of different ages spent attending to toys, followed by an examination of changes in children's frequency of activities at different levels of play sophistication. These cross-age changes in play are based on ten minutes of alone play. Reported results are based on repeated-measures analyses of variance across age; these were followed by post hoc pairwise comparisons where overall F values were significant.

Duration. Total duration of attending to the toys did not change across age. However, when attention measures were considered in the context of the actions that children exhibited while attending, notable developmental changes were observed. Duration of looking without tactual manipulation decreased between five and nine months and then reached an asymptote. For both examining and effects, children peaked at nine months and declined thereafter.

Level. Frequencies of nonsymbolic and symbolic play showed somewhat different patterns of change. Children's nonsymbolic play increased steadily from five to thirteen months and then showed a marginal decrease at seventeen months. Further analysis indicated that the decline in nonsymbolic play is explained by a specific drop in the lowest level of symbolic play (that is, unitary functional activity), rather than a global decline in the frequency of all types of nonsymbolic play (see Tamis-LeMonda and Bornstein, 1991). In contrast, frequencies of children's symbolic play steadily increased between nine and seventeen months. (This sort of play was nonexistent at five months.)

Are the Two Indexes of Play Associated with One Another?

We next assessed links between individual differences in children's duration and level in play. As anticipated, concurrent associations between duration and level in play were identified at different ages. At both nine and thirteen months, more attention in play was associated with a greater number of nonsymbolic and symbolic play acts. At seventeen months, more attending was associated with a greater number of symbolic acts only. This accords with the finding that by seventeen months children are dropping certain nonsymbolic levels of play from their repertoires. Elsewhere, we have shown that children's sustained overall attention also relates to their symbolic play (Tamis-LeMonda and Bornstein, 1990). Thus, variation among children in attention in play is associated with variation among children in sophistication in play from infancy through the middle of the second year, suggesting that measures of play duration and play level might reflect a common underlying ability in children.

How Do the Two Indexes of Play Relate to Other Mental Abilities in the Child?

Our next analyses examined links between the two indexes of play, on the one hand, and indexes of language, on the other. Parallels in the development of play and language, as well as associations between the two, have suggested to many that a core component of *representational ability* might underlie the development of play and language. However, most play-language analyses have focused on play level rather than duration. We sought to confirm the level-to-language association, to extend these findings to duration, and to do so for various measures of language across several ages in early development. Analyses were based on children's collaborative play with mothers.

At thirteen months, children's receptive language was associated with the frequency of their symbolic play ($r = .34$, $p < .05$), but not the duration of sustained overall attention ($r = .10$) or total attention ($r = .12$). These correlations partial mothers' stimulation from both play and language.

In the same cohort of children, thirteen- and twenty-one-month frequency of symbolic play related to language production at twenty-one months. Play level at the start of the second year predicted later language, and later play level related concurrently to language. However, these relations were specific. Both thirteen- and twenty-one-month frequency of symbolic play were associated with twenty-one-month semantic diversity (r's = .44 and .48, respectively; p's < .01), but not with productive vocabulary size or grammar as assessed by MLU (r's range from .07 to .24, p's > .10). Both concurrent and predictive associations between play level and language remained after covarying mothers' contributions to both language and play (partial r's = .38 and .41, respectively; p's < .01). Together, these data suggest that associations between toddler play and language are specific to measures of play sophistication and to aspects of language having to do with meaning. The fact that play-language links are not mediated by maternal stimulation further suggests that they reflect a core underlying component of representation *in the child* (see also Bornstein, Vibbert, Tal, and O'Donnell, 1992; Tamis-LeMonda and Bornstein, 1989, 1990; Vibbert and Bornstein, 1989).

What Are the Infant Antecedents of Duration and Level in Play?

In a separate series of studies, we have examined links between spontaneous activity and information processing in infancy, on the one hand, and duration and level of toddler play, on the other.

Infant Activity as a Predictor. We first examined prediction from infants' behaviors during alone play at five months to alone play at thirteen months. Because five-month-olds do not engage in either nonsymbolic or symbolic play, our analyses focused on babies' overall attention and attention during examining and producing effects. We found a marginal degree of stability: Specifically, five-month sustained overall attention and production of effects each predicted thirteen-month sustained overall attention (r's = .31 and .35, respectively; p's < .10). Predictive correlations from five-month duration of attention in play to thirteen-month level of sophistication in play showed that infants who sustained attention for greater periods of time at five months, particularly while examining objects or producing effects, engaged in more nonsymbolic and symbolic play. In addition, exploratory analyses showed a relation between five-month sustained attention and thirteen-month sustained attention in nonsymbolic and in symbolic play (significant r's range from .32 to .66).

Infant Habituation as a Predictor. The next set of analyses explored associations between infant habituation and toddler duration and level in play, after covarying mothers' earlier and later stimulation from dependent and independent measures in the child. In addition, maternal IQ served as a covariate. (IQ has been found to covary with infant habituation; Bornstein and Tamis-LeMonda, 1992.) Infant habituation predicted both sustained overall attention ($r = -.26$, $p < .10$) and frequency of symbolic play ($r = -.32$, $p < .05$), over and above maternal contributions as well as stability in activity from infancy to the second year. Only the link to play level achieved the accepted level of significance, however.

Infant Activity and Habituation as Predictors of Toddler Exploratory Competence. Quantitative and qualitative measures of play, although treated separately, covary in the child and together might provide a more comprehensive picture of children's exploratory competencies. Our final analyses examined the two measures together in terms of *exploratory competence,* a latent factor reflecting the unique variance shared by sustained overall duration and level in play, and assessed infant antecedents of toddler exploratory competence. We examined the unique and joint prediction of the two infant antecedents—spontaneous activity and habituation—with respect to this factor. Prediction from infant measures was again assessed after covarying mothers' IQ and stimulation. As shown in Figure 2.1, exploratory competence was uniquely predicted by each of the two infant antecedents. Specifically, five-month-olds whose peak look was shorter and who engaged in more vocal and exploratory activities were more competent explorers at thirteen months. This analysis documents stability from infant performance to toddler attention and sophistication in play. Moreover, stability in infants maintains over and above the contributions of their mothers. ———————

Conclusion

Toddler play can be assessed quantitatively and qualitatively. Qualitative measures typically focus on the contents of children's actions with objects, as, for example, by asking about the relative sophistication of a pretense activity and its amount. The outcome of such a conceptualization has been

Figure 2.1. Infant Predictors
of Toddler Exploratory Competence

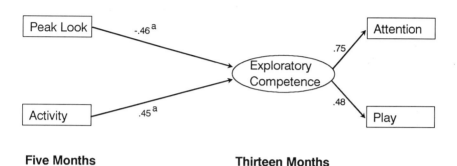

Five Months   **Thirteen Months**

Note: This figure illustrates unique predictions from infant habituation (peak look) and infant home activity to toddler exploratory competence over and above maternal stimulation and IQ. Predictive paths present partial correlations; $\chi^2(2) = 1.57$, $p = .46$, goodness-of-fit index = .94.

[a]$p < .01$

the classification of play into a progressive series of developmental levels. Quantitative measures of play focus on the duration of activity, regardless of content, as, for example, by asking how long children play at some act. In this chapter, we distinguish duration of attention from level of sophistication in play, note characteristics of these two indexes, and explore associations between them and other mental abilities in the infant and toddler.

Over the first two years, children add examination to visual attention, and they add symbolic play to nonsymbolic play. Moreover, children change in the way that they distribute their attention across levels of play sophistication.

We have found consistent relations between duration and level in play across various time periods in early development. One interpretation of their shared variance is that the two indexes are subserved by a common underlying construct, perhaps exploratory competence. However, these relations between the quantitative and qualitative aspects of play are only moderate, and the two show different relations to other measures of the child. For example, frequency of symbolic play is more strongly related to language than is duration of play. This suggests that play sophistication in particular, like language, might reflect an underlying representational competence in children.

Attention in early infancy during alone play predicts both attention and sophistication in toddler play. This relative stability underscores the probable role of one index, attention, in the development of another, sophistication. One interpretation of these findings is that the ability to stay on task might be a necessary, if alone insufficient, precursor of higher levels of play. Other cognitive factors, particularly the ability to represent past experience, might also be requisite to the achievement of higher play levels. Similarly, habituation in infancy predicts toddler play, as well as the latent construct of exploratory competence. Specifically, those infants exhibiting shorter peak looks during habituation later engaged in more symbolic play and longer durations of sustained overall attention. Notably, the two infant antecedents of later play, activity and habituation, revealed different patterns of prediction. Whereas measures of infant attending in naturalistic conditions correlated positively with later attention and sophistication in play, attention during laboratory habituation was inversely related to these measures. These contrasting patterns imply that the infant's task during free play differs from the infant's task during habituation, that is, attention in one setting differs functionally from attention in the other. Brief looks during the habituation procedure might index faster processing and thus reflect a more efficient attention pattern. In contrast, in situations such as free play that permit toddlers to explore more actively, sustained interest, particularly at higher levels, seems to index greater competence (see also Ruff and Saltarelli, this volume).

When discussing developmental changes and variability in toddler play, some researchers have emphasized the cognitive-representational nature of play (for example, Ungerer and Sigman, 1984). Others have focused on motivation and goal-directedness in play, thought to be evidenced in toddlers' sustaining and regulating attention (for example, Power, Chapieski, and McGrath, 1985). Empirically, we distinguish two indexes of play, duration and level, that map onto these conceptually distinct yet interdependent aspects of play. Moreover, we show that both components are multiply predicted by mental functions in infancy and relate differentially to mental functions in early childhood. Untangling the web of these interrelations points the way for the task of further plumbing the mind of the young child.

Note

1. Our classification of play distinguishes nonsymbolic play from symbolic play. Symbolic play is considered higher in level than nonsymbolic play; this classification depends somewhat on available materials. We provide toys that do not afford children the opportunity for complex constructive play. Constructive play, although often nonsymbolic in nature, is more sophisticated than the exploratory types of nonsymbolic play that we coded. Hence, developmentally, nonsymbolic activity appears prior to symbolic; in contrast, constructive play ought to be considered different from, but not less sophisticated than, symbolic play.

References

Bates, E., Bretherton, I., Shore, C., and McNew, S. "Names, Gestures and Objects: Symbolization in Infancy and Aphasia." In K. Nelson (ed.), *Children's Language.* Vol. 4. Hillsdale, N.J.: Erlbaum, 1983.

Bates, E., Bretherton, I., and Snyder, L. *From First Words to Grammar: Individual Differences and Dissociable Mechanisms.* New York: Cambridge University Press, 1988.

Bates, E., O'Connell, B., and Shore, C. "Language and Communication in Infancy." In J. D. Osofsky (ed.), *Handbook of Infant Development.* (2nd ed.) New York: Wiley, 1987.

Belsky, J., Goode, M. K., and Most, R. K. "Maternal Stimulation and Infant Exploratory Competence: Cross-Sectional, Correlational, and Experimental Analyses." *Child Development,* 1980, *51,* 1163–1178.

Belsky, J., and Most, R. K. "From Exploration to Play: A Cross-Sectional Study of Infant Free-Play Behavior." *Developmental Psychology,* 1981, *17,* 630–639.

Bornstein, M. H., and Sigman, M. D. "Continuity in Mental Development from Infancy." *Child Development,* 1986, *57,* 251–274.

Bornstein, M. H., and Tamis-LeMonda, C. S. "Activities and Interactions of Mothers and Their Firstborn Infants in the First Six Months of Life: Covariation, Stability, Continuity, Correspondence, and Prediction." *Child Development,* 1990, *61,* 1206–1217.

Bornstein, M. H., and Tamis-LeMonda, C. S. "Origins of Cognitive Skills in Infants." Unpublished manuscript, National Institute of Child Health and Human Development, 1992.

Bornstein, M. H., Vibbert, M., Tal, J., and O'Donnell, K. "Toddler Language and Play in the Second Year: Stability, Covariation, and Influences of Parenting." *First Language,* 1992, *12,* 323–338.

Dixon, W. E., and Shore, C. "What Shall We Play? Play Content as a Vehicle for Parent-Infant Interactions." *Infant Behavior and Development,* in press.

Fein, G. G. "Pretend Play in Childhood: An Integrated Review." *Child Development,* 1981, *52,* 1095–1118.

Fenson, L., and others. *Technical Manual for the MacArthur Communicative Development Inventories.* San Diego: San Diego State University, 1991.

McCune-Nicolich, L. "Toward Symbolic Functioning: Structure of Early Pretend Games and Potential Parallels with Language." *Child Development,* 1981, *52,* 785–797.

Piaget, J. *Play, Dreams, and Imitation in Childhood.* New York: Norton, 1962.

Power, T. G., Chapieski, M. L., and McGrath, M. P. "Assessment of Individual Differences in Infant Exploration and Play." *Developmental Psychology,* 1985, *21,* 974–981.

Rubin, K. H., Fein, G. G., and Vandenberg, B. "Play." In P. Mussen (ed.), *Handbook of Child Psychology.* New York: Wiley, 1983.

Tamis-LeMonda, C. S., and Bornstein, M. H. "Habituation and Maternal Encouragement of Attention in Infancy as Predictors of Toddler Language, Play, and Representational Competence." *Child Development,* 1989, *60,* 738–751.

Tamis-LeMonda, C. S., and Bornstein, M. H. "Language, Play, and Attention at One Year." *Infant Behavior and Development,* 1990, *13,* 85–98.

Tamis-LeMonda, C. S., and Bornstein, M. H. "Individual Variation, Correspondence, Stability, and Change in Mother and Toddler Play." *Infant Behavior and Development,* 1991, *14,* 143–162.

Ungerer, J. A., and Sigman, M. D. "The Relation of Play and Sensorimotor Behavior to Language in the Second Year." *Child Development,* 1984, *55,* 1440–1455.

Vibbert, M., and Bornstein, M. H. "Specific Associations Between Domains of Mother-Child Interaction and Toddler Referential Language and Pretense Play." *Infant Behavior and Development,* 1989, *12,* 163–184.

CATHERINE S. TAMIS-LEMONDA is assistant professor of psychology, Department of Applied Psychology, New York University. Her research focuses on cognitive and perceptual development in infancy, language, and play in early childhood; parent-child interactions; and cross-cultural comparisons of early dyadic interactions.

MARC H. BORNSTEIN is senior research scientist and head of Child and Family Research at the National Institute of Child Health and Human Development, Bethesda, Maryland. His interests include experimental, methodological, comparative, developmental, cross-cultural, and aesthetic psychology.

*This chapter presents a synthesis of empirical research supporting use
of observation of children's play as a cognitive assessment tool. In
addition, the relation between specific deficits in play and diagnosis of
developmental disabilities is discussed.*

Pretend Play in High-Risk and Developmentally Delayed Children

Marian Sigman, Rhonda Sena

During solitary and social play, children demonstrate interest in their
environment and make use of the representational abilities available to
them. For this reason, observations of the play behaviors of children
provide an opportunity to evaluate both their interest in exploration and
their symbolic understanding. Because children will play relatively un-self-
consciously in many settings, play offers a way to determine which representational schemes children understand as well as the thematic issues that
interest them. In this chapter, we discuss the use of observations of
children's play as a means of evaluating children's exploratory and cognitive capacities. To narrow the topic, we focus on the intensity and level of
play behaviors of children in the first to third years of development,
concentrating on solitary rather than social play. In addition, we emphasize the structural forms of play, which indicate children's symbolic
understanding, rather than the themes of play, which evidence their
concerns and interests.

Individual differences can be identified in two aspects of object play.

Work described in this chapter was supported by grants NS25243 and HD17662 from
the National Institute of Neurological Diseases and Strokes and National Institute of
Child Health and Human Development, respectively, and by the U.S. Agency for
International Development contract DAN1309-G-SS-80. We thank Peter Mundy and
Judy Ungerer for their collaboration in the work on preterm infants and developmentally delayed children. Charlotte Neumann and Nimrod Bwibo facilitated the studies
of play of Kenyan children. This chapter was written while the senior author was in
residence at the MRC Cognitive Development Unit, London, England.

First, observations can be used to determine the extent to which the infant sustains attention to objects (Jennings and others, 1979; Krakow, Kopp, and Vaughn, 1981). Second, the level of symbolic representation can be assessed by measuring the extent to which play is dominated by more sophisticated forms of object use (Belsky and Most, 1981; Bretherton and Bates, 1984; Tamis-LeMonda and Bornstein, 1989). Play competence, then, can be considered to reflect two different underlying mental capacities—exploratory competence and representational competence—that may have different origins, correlates, and consequences (Tamis-LeMonda and Bornstein, 1990).

There are two aims of using play as an early cognitive assessment technique. First, play observations can be used for the identification of cognitive disorders in normal and high-risk infants. To the extent that play accurately reflects the interests and representational abilities of infants, deficits in these interests and abilities can be uncovered and become the focus of early intervention. A major research question, then, is whether the symbol forms that children use in play reflect their general level of representation. The strongest support for this notion is that children who use more advanced forms of play concurrently use more advanced forms of language. The evidence that more advanced play at one age predicts more advanced language or cognitive skills later in the child's life is mixed. This chapter reviews available evidence for the generality and predictability of play skills with particular reference to high-risk and developmentally disabled populations.

Play observations are also used as an aid in understanding developmental disorders. Observations of early play skills have been utilized to determine whether exploratory or symbolic capacities are specifically impaired in children suffering from various developmental disabilities. Moreover, since children with different developmental disabilities manifest different amounts and levels of pretend play, play observations can be used for diagnosis of individual children.

Developmental Progression in Play

One of the advantages of using play as an assessment technique is its universality. However, the universality of play is only an advantage if similar developmental progressions occur across gender, socioeconomic, and cultural groups. Most studies identify a similar developmental progression in all cultures. The simple manipulation of objects manifested in early infancy is succeeded by relational play in which the infant combines objects by stacking them, lining them up, hitting one against another, and placing one within another. At thirteen to fourteen months of age, infants make functional use of objects in play (sometimes called self- and other-directed pretense), such as combing the hair of a doll with a hairbrush. At about twenty months, the infant engages in truly symbolic play such as pretending that one object is another, carrying out actions with imaginary objects, or attributing characteristics to an object that it does not possess. For example, the child may attribute animacy to a doll so that the doll carries out actions of its own.

The distinction between functional and symbolic play is central to the discussion in this chapter. An example of functional play is the child brushing the hair of a doll or a parent. An example of symbolic play is the child pretending that a doll looks in a mirror or the child feeding the parent from an imaginary glass. Symbolic play has greater cognitive requirements than does functional play in that the child is representing truly imaginary objects and activities rather than simply reproducing observed conventional acts using real objects in the play setting. For this reason, some theorists see symbolic play as a manifestation of metarepresentational abilities not required in functional play (Baron-Cohen, 1987; Leslie, 1987).

Most studies of play development find a similar progression even in nonindustrialized countries with cultures very different from those of the United States and Western Europe. For example, in a comparison of the play behaviors of mother-child dyads in Mexico and the United States, Farver and Howes (in press) reported that thirty-six-month-olds in both countries showed a greater proportion of symbolic play than did eighteen-month-olds. Similarly, in a longitudinal study of fifteen- to thirty-month-olds observed every other month in rural Kenya, the total amount of play remained stable across the period but the percentage of simple manipulation and relational play declined while the percentage of symbolic play increased (Sigman and others, 1988).

Individual Differences and Their Consequences in High-Risk Infants

Infants may vary in their play behaviors in ways that reflect their individual experiences and development. Children whose development is placed at risk because of complicating birth conditions or early deprivation are of particular interest in this regard.

Play in Preterm Infants. Studies of infants whose development is placed at risk because of preterm birth are useful for several reasons. First, the study of preterm infants can help to determine whether stages of play emerge as a function of maturation or environmental input. Second, the range of variation in abilities at any age is generally greater with high-risk infants than with low-risk infants. Although the majority of preterm infants show normal development throughout their lives, a greater percentage of preterm infants than full-term infants have intelligence in the borderline or mentally retarded range (IQs below 85). The greater heterogeneity of the preterm group enhances the possibility of predictive relations between variables. Moreover, the heterogeneity of the group is part of the justification for studying play as an early form of cognitive representation. The aim of these studies is to identify those children whose symbolic development is slow so that early intervention can be implemented.

Exploratory Competence. A number of studies have shown less exploratory competence in high-risk preterm infants than in full-term infants (Morgan, Maslin-Cole, Biringin, and Harmon, 1991). Compared to full-term infants, preterm infants explore novel objects less (Sigman, 1976), examine objects less (Ruff, 1988), shift focus of attention between a number of objects less, and look at fewer objects, although the duration of attention to objects is similar for the two groups (Landry, Chapieski, Fletcher, and Denson, 1988). The extent to which the infants shifted gaze was associated with later development for the highest risk group in the study by Landry, Chapieski, Fletcher, and Denson (1988). Several studies suggest that a disturbance in attention regulation also appears in children with Down syndrome (Krakow and Kopp, 1983; Landry and Chapieski, 1989; MacTurk and others, 1985). Thus, this disturbance in attention deployment may be a general marker of cognitive delay. Preterm infants who experience serious medical complications show different exploration patterns from those of full-term infants, but preterm infants who have fewer complications and develop more normally demonstrate exploration patterns that are generally appropriate for their corrected age (Landry, Chapieski, and Schmidt, 1986; Ruff, Lawson, Parrinello, and Weissberg, 1990; Sigman, 1976; Ungerer and Sigman, 1983).

Representational Competence. Representational competence developed largely as a function of biological maturity in a study of the play behaviors of a group of preterm infants tested at thirteen and one-half and twenty-two months postnatal and corrected ages (Ungerer and Sigman, 1983). In this study, age was calculated from birth, disregarding preterm birth, in the first observation and from gestation in the second observation. The full-term control group was observed twice, with testing sessions separated by one to two weeks. Full-term infants performed a greater number of functional and symbolic acts and more play sequences than did preterm infants of the same postnatal age. However, there were no differences when the infants were tested at ages corrected for differences in the length of gestation. At twenty-two months, the preterm infants continued to perform fewer symbolic acts and more simple manipulation when the length of the gestational period was ignored in calculating age. There were no differences between the corrected-age-matched groups. Thus, play appears to develop largely as a function of maturation, although cross-cultural research (see Wachs, this volume) does implicate environmental influences as well.

Concurrent and Predictive Correlates of Play. Representational play appears to index general symbolic understanding in that level of play is concurrently and predictively associated with language skills in both preterm and full-term infants (Ungerer and Sigman, 1984). Play and language skills were concurrently and predictively associated for the preterm and full-term samples discussed above. Although the associations were stronger for the preterm sample than for the full-term sample, the correlations were not statistically different for the two groups. Children at thirteen and one-half months who engaged in a greater number of doll-directed and other-directed functional play acts and used more sequences of three or more related functional acts (such as removing the doll's hat, brushing her hair, and putting her in the crib) had higher language scores at the same age and at twenty-two months of age. Symbolic play (that is, play involving substitute or imaginary objects) was also concurrently related to language abilities at twenty-two months.

One play measure, the amount of relational play (in which objects are simply combined by stacking or putting one within another) at twenty-two months, was negatively related to language abilities at the same age and negatively associated with general intelligence level when the children reached five years of age. The twenty-two-month-old preterm and full-term infants who spent a considerable proportion of their play time in simple combining of objects rather than in functional or symbolic play were less intelligent five-year-olds than infants who were less occupied with simple combining of objects (McDonald, Sigman, and Ungerer, 1989). The duration of relational play added to the prediction of intelligence at five years of age even when scores on a developmental scale administered at twenty-two months were considered.

Play in Mildly Malnourished Infants. Because play is exhibited universally, it is a potentially useful tool in observations of toddlers in different cultures. However, it must be kept in mind that children's play should be observed in familiar circumstances. In order to do this in a study conducted in rural Kenya, we used bimonthly observations of play behaviors in which the toddlers engaged either alone or with others during two-hour periods. Both exploratory and representational competence were correlated with the level of nutrition and verbal stimulation provided for this group of eighteen- to thirty-month-olds (Sigman and others, 1988, 1989). Infants who were well fed and talked to more frequently by caregivers and siblings engaged in more total play over the year and more symbolic play at thirty months than did less well nourished and verbally stimulated infants. Despite the sensitivity of play to environmental influences, play behaviors did not predict general cognitive abilities at age five years in this sample (Sigman, McDonald, Neumann, and Bwibo, 1991). Associations between play abilities and later language skills have not been investigated as yet in this sample.

Play in Children with Developmental Disabilities

Observations of the play behaviors of children with disabilities can shed light on the nature of the disabilities. It is important to know whether exploratory and representational abilities are specifically impaired as a result of the developmental disorder. Moreover, many children with disabilities have limited capacities to express themselves verbally. Play observations often allow one to see a bit more into the minds of these children than would be possible with sole reliance on verbal exchange. Finally, play observations can be of use in differentiating one diagnostic condition from another since exploratory and representational competencies vary across developmental disabilities.

Play in Children with Down Syndrome. Exploratory and representational competence have been assessed in children with Down syndrome.

Exploratory Competence. Exploratory competence appears to be deficient in children with Down syndrome, although the definition of this deficiency varies from one study to the next. In terms of quality of object exploration, children with Down syndrome have been shown to spend more time involved in visual exploration and less time involved in manual exploration than exhibited by normal control subjects matched on chronological or mental age (Vietze and others, 1983). In some studies, children with Down syndrome play with toys less than do other developmentally delayed and normal children (Brooks-Gunn and Lewis, 1982; Krakow and Kopp, 1983). Thus, the results point to either a deficiency in exploratory competence or a lack of interest in object mastery (Ruskin, Mundy, Kasari, and Sigman, 1992).

Representational Competence. In contrast to exploratory competence, children with Down syndrome demonstrate representational competence commensurate with their general cognitive level (Baron-Cohen, 1987; Beeghly, Perry, and Cicchetti, 1989; Hill and McCune-Nicolich, 1981; Motti, Cicchetti, and Sroufe, 1983). There are, however, some differences in the play of children with Down syndrome as compared to mental-age-matched controls. Weiss, Beeghly, and Cicchetti (1985) measured children's average and highest levels of symbolic play. Children with Down syndrome were found to have significantly lower average scores on play scales compared to mental-age-matched controls, possibly because these children tended to repeat the same schemes more often than did nonretarded children. This perseveration would seem to reflect a disorder in the way in which objects are focused on or manipulated rather than a disorder in representational understanding.

Play in Mentally Retarded Children. Mentally retarded children without Down syndrome have exploratory and representational competencies similar to normal children of equivalent mental age. In two of our studies, the durations and distributions of play acts of the mentally retarded children were similar to or even more advanced than those of the normal children who were matched to them on mental age. Thus, the mentally retarded children appeared to explore and play with objects in much the same way as the normal children.

Play in Autistic Children. The development of symbolic play has been of great interest to researchers and clinicians in the United States and Great Britain.

Exploratory Competence. In contrast to mentally retarded children, the play of autistic children is markedly different from that of children of similar developmental abilities. In general, studies have focused on representational competence rather than exploratory competence. However, some studies have shown less exploration of objects depending on the setting. In unstructured situations, autistic children frequently explore objects less than do control subjects (Hermelin and O'Connor, 1970; Kasari, Sigman, and Yirmiya, 1992). When parents, experimenters, or teachers actively encourage object exploration by limiting the space in which the child can move and by handing objects to the child, object exploration increases and becomes equivalent to that shown by normal and mentally retarded children of the same developmental level. The exception to this is doll play, where even adult participation fails to engage autistic children to the same degree as it does control children (Sigman, Mundy, Sherman, and Ungerer, 1986).

Representational Competence. Early studies of symbolic play in autistic children demonstrated a paucity of representational play acts (Tilton and Ottinger, 1964; Weiner, Ottinger, and Tilton, 1969). A subsequent study using developmentally based definitions of play and control groups demonstrated that autistic children engaged in less pretend play than exhibited by mentally retarded and normal children (Wing, Gould, Yeates, and Brierly, 1977). More recent studies have differentiated play more precisely and have varied the amount of structure provided for the children's play activities (Baron-Cohen, 1987; Mundy, Sigman, Ungerer, and Sherman, 1986; Riquet, Taylor, Benroya, and Klein, 1981; Sigman and Ungerer, 1984).

The evidence for a deficit in functional play is mixed. In one study, a group of sixteen autistic children showed less functional play in both unstructured and structured situations than a group of sixteen mentally retarded children matched on mental and chronological age and a group of sixteen normal children matched on mental age (Sigman and Ungerer, 1984). In the unstructured situation in which the child was placed in a room with a variety of toys after a few functional acts had been modeled, the autistic children engaged in less functional play and fewer sequences of three or more related functional acts than the children in the other groups. The autistic children directed functional play acts to another person or a doll less than exhibited by the children in the other groups.

They also performed less diverse play in that they demonstrated a smaller number of different functional acts. In the structured situation, objects in a toy set were presented to the child one at a time or in small groups of related items by an experimenter who recorded spontaneous uses. The autistic children produced fewer different doll-directed functional acts as well as fewer different functional acts in general.

One British study has replicated these findings and another has not. Baron-Cohen (1987) studied a group of older, more advanced autistic children and did not find differences in functional play in an unstructured situation when these children were compared to control groups matched on verbal mental age. With a sample even more developmentally advanced, Lewis and Boucher (1988) studied play in both structured and unstructured situations. The autistic children had language abilities in the four- to five-year-old age range, and the control groups were matched on these language abilities. In the unstructured situation, the autistic children engaged in functional play less than the other two groups, although all but two of the autistic children engaged in at least some functional play.

The basis for the variation in results is not clear. One explanation is that the differences in functional play are a result of differing language skills between the groups. In line with this hypothesis, we did not find significant differences in functional play when we repeated this study with new samples of children who were matched on both mental and verbal abilities. On the other hand, in the first study, the mentally retarded children who did not show evidence of language comprehension still demonstrated more functional play than the autistic children who appeared to understand words. Thus, diagnosis seemed more important than receptive language abilities. The explanation that functional play differences among groups are found only when the groups are not matched on language abilities also does not account for the difference observed in the study by Lewis and Boucher (1988) in which the autistic and control groups were matched on language competence.

All of our studies have shown fewer symbolic play acts by autistic children than by control children. In one study (Sigman and Ungerer, 1984), autistic children showed less diverse symbolic play acts in both the unstructured and structured situations, although both functional and symbolic play were enhanced by structuring of the situation. The number of symbolic acts performed in the structured situation was also lower for the autistic children in our second study in which the children were matched on both mental and verbal abilities (Mundy, Sigman, Ungerer, and Sherman, 1986). Preliminary results from a current study suggest differences in symbolic play in the structured situation like those reported previously. In line with these findings, Baron-Cohen (1987) found that significantly fewer autistic children produced any spontaneous symbolic play relative to the normal and retarded control groups. Only two autistic children demonstrated any pretend play, whereas only two children with Down syndrome and one normal child showed a complete lack of spontaneous symbolic play acts.

To summarize, a large number of studies have documented deficiencies in symbolic play in young autistic children with language abilities in the eighteen- to twenty-five-month-old range even when these children are matched on language abilities with the mentally retarded children. Only the study by Lewis and Boucher (1988) has failed to find differences in symbolic play. In their unstructured situation, very few of the children in any group performed spontaneous symbolic play, which suggests that the toys or the situation were inappropriate for this age group. In the structured situation, there were also no group differences. All of the autistic children produced some symbolic play acts by making one object stand for another or imagining absent objects to be present. This study clearly demonstrates that autistic children who achieve language abilities comparable to five-year-olds are able to use symbols in play, but the evidence for a lack of group differences is unconvincing. Five-year-olds' pretend play is likely to be inhibited by the presence of an unfamiliar adult (particularly if also an interfering adult) and usually is carried out with peers. For this reason, the play measure may have been developmentally inappropriate so that the diversity of symbolic play acts of the normal and mentally retarded children was diminished in both the unstructured and structured situations.

Concurrent Associations Between Play and Language Skills in Children with Disabilities. In line with the findings on normal and preterm infants discussed above, there are significant associations between play and language skills in mentally retarded and autistic groups. In our first study, we found significant associations between receptive language skills and the number of more advanced play acts for all groups. For example, normal children who showed more functional and symbolic play acts in both structured and unstructured situations could comprehend more language. Mentally retarded children who performed more symbolic play acts in both situations were similarly more advanced in language comprehension. It is noteworthy that play skills were not associated with language production skills in both the normal and mentally retarded groups. Tamis-LeMonda and Bornstein (1990) also reported concurrent associations between play and receptive language skills at thirteen months but not between play and language production skills. At twenty months, receptive language skills were not measured; play skills were correlated with pragmatic diversity but not with productive vocabulary size or mean length of utterance (Tamis-LeMonda and Bornstein, 1992).

For the autistic children, both receptive and expressive language skills were associated with the number of functional play acts and sequences of three or more acts in the unstructured situation as well as with the number of functional and symbolic play acts in the structured situation. Language production skills were probably associated with play skills for the autistic children and not for the other two groups because of the greater overlap in receptive and expressive language skills for the autistic children. Normal and mentally retarded children tend to have a greater divergence between their expressive and receptive language abilities than is true for autistic children at this age level.

Doll-directed play appears to be a specific correlate of language acquisition. Autistic children who gave no indication of understanding language also engaged in few functional doll-directed acts as well as less symbolic play in the structured situations. These findings were replicated in a subsequent study in which the total number of doll-directed functional and symbolic play acts were significantly associated with receptive language age scores. Moreover, doll-directed play was specifically associated with language for the mentally retarded children. The four mentally retarded children in the first study who gave no indication of understanding language also utilized less doll-directed functional play than the twelve mentally retarded children who demonstrated language comprehension.

Conclusion

In the introduction, we suggested that pretend play can be useful as an assessment tool only if certain requirements are met. First, both exploratory and representational competence must develop along parallel lines in different environments and cultures, and this appears to be the case. Second, exploratory and representational competence must both concurrently and predictively index other core abilities in the infant. Exploratory competence appears to predict later cognitive abilities in high-risk and disabled groups. Representational competence is tightly associated with language skills, particularly language comprehension, both concurrently and during the period in which language is being acquired. Play, then, may be practically useful for identifying the symbolic competence of a child, particularly one who is reluctant to speak to or in front of an unfamiliar adult.

There is little evidence that representational competence as measured in play observations predicts general intellectual abilities in normal and high-risk infants. An exception may be that children who fail to replace simple manipulation and combinatorial play with functional and symbolic play may be at risk for intellectual delay. Finally, play observations differentiate children who suffer from risk conditions and children who have not experienced such risk events.

In an even more specific way, play observations are useful for distinguishing among the characteristics of children with different forms of disabilities. Mentally retarded children show little difficulty with play, although children with Down syndrome seem to explore objects somewhat less avidly and less flexibly than do normal children. The symbolic play skills of language-delayed children who are not autistic are comparable to or a bit better than their language skills. Autistic children show the most profound disturbance of any group in both representational play and language. Thus, autistic children whose play and language skills are lower than their mental ages can be distinguished from mentally retarded children who have play and language skills close to their mental ages and from language-delayed children who have play but not language skills close to their mental ages.

The paucity of flexible symbolic play has been seen as a core characteristic of autism. Some researchers think that the deficit in symbolic play is part of a metarepresentational disorder, because truly symbolic play, particularly in interaction with another person, may require the ability to understand that other people have attitudes about the world (Leslie, 1988). Others believe that metarepresentation is not necessary for pretend play, although secondary representation, in which the child can deal with real and hypothetical situations, is required (Perner, 1991). Hence, autism is not seen to involve a metarepresentational deficit in this view. Finally, some researchers question the pervasiveness of the play deficit because of evidence that verbally autistic children do understand some symbolic play acts (Harris, in press).

In fact, the ubiquity of the play deficit in young autistic children is remarkable. The failure of autistic children to show the spontaneous, elaborated play scenarios demonstrated by children, even mentally retarded children, in all cultures suggests that the limitation in representational competence is a core deficit. In our view, play is impaired in autistic children because pretend play requires social observation and knowledge as well as symbolic understanding that are critically and specifically deficient in autistic children (Sigman, in press).

The final use suggested for play observations is in diagnosis. In clinical practice, a quick way to rule out the diagnosis of autism is to observe spontaneous, exuberant pretend play in a child and little preoccupation with lining up objects or spinning the wheels of cars and trucks. These observations are readily made by teachers and parents who frequently comment on the presence or absence of pretend play with no prompting from professionals. Although it may make sense from a research perspective to match autistic and mentally retarded groups on language abilities, language acquisition is delayed in autistic children as compared to mentally retarded children. Since play and language are so highly associated, the equating of groups on language skills obfuscates the differences in play that are so clinically useful in differentiating between groups who, by definition, have different symbolic skills.

References

Baron-Cohen, S. "Autism and Symbolic Play." *British Journal of Developmental Psychology,* 1987, *5,* 139–148.

Beeghly, M., Perry, B. W., and Cicchetti, D. "Structural and Affective Dimensions of Play Development in Young Children with Down Syndrome." *International Journal of Behavioral Development,* 1989, *12,* 257–277.

Belsky, J., and Most, R. K. "From Exploration to Play: A Cross-Sectional Study of Infant Free-Play Behavior." *Developmental Psychology,* 1981, *17,* 630–639.

Bretherton, I., and Bates, E. "The Development of Representation from 10 to 28 Months: Differential Stability of Language and Symbolic Play." In R. N. Emde and R. J. Harmon (eds.), *Continuities and Discontinuities in Development.* New York: Plenum, 1984.

Brooks-Gunn, J., and Lewis, M. "Affective Exchanges Between Normal and Handicapped Infants and Their Mothers." In T. Field and A. Fogel (eds.), *Emotion and Interaction: Normal and High-Risk Infants.* Hillsdale, N.J.: Erlbaum, 1982.

Farver, J. M., and Howes, C. A. "Cultural Differences in American and Mexican Pretend Play." *Merrill-Palmer Quarterly,* in press.

Harris, P. L. "Pretending and Planning." In S. Baron-Cohen, H. Tager-Flusberg, and D. Cohen (eds.), *Understanding Other Minds: Perspectives from Autism.* Oxford, England: Oxford University Press, in press.

Hermelin, B., and O'Connor, N. *Psychological Experiments with Autistic Children.* Elmsford, N.Y.: Pergamon Press, 1970.

Hill, P. M., and McCune-Nicolich, L. "Pretend Play and Patterns of Cognition in Down's Syndrome Children." *Child Development,* 1981, *52,* 611–617.

Jennings, K. D., and others. "Exploratory Play as an Index of Mastery Motivation: Relationships to Persistence, Cognitive Functioning, and Environmental Measures." *Developmental Psychology,* 1979, *15,* 386–394.

Kasari, C., Sigman, M. D., and Yirmiya, N. "Focused and Social Attention in Interactions with Familiar and Unfamiliar Adults: A Comparison of Autistic, Mentally Retarded, and Normal Children." Unpublished manuscript, University of California, Los Angeles, 1992.

Krakow, J. B., and Kopp, C. B. "The Effects of Developmental Delay on Sustained Attention in Young Children." *Child Development,* 1983, *54,* 1143–1155.

Krakow, J. B., Kopp, C. B., and Vaughn, B. E. "Sustained Attention in Young Children." Paper presented at the biennial meeting of the Society for Research in Child Development, Boston, April 1981.

Landry, S. H., and Chapieski, M. L. "Joint Attention and Infant Toy Exploration: Effects of Down Syndrome and Prematurity." *Child Development,* 1989, *60,* 103–119.

Landry, S. H., Chapieski, M. L., Fletcher, J., and Denson, S. "Three-Year Outcome for Low Birth Weight Infants: Differential Effects of Early Medical Complications." *Journal of Pediatric Psychology,* 1988, *13,* 317–327.

Landry, S. H., Chapieski, M. L., and Schmidt, M. "Effects of Maternal Attention Directing Strategies on Preterms' Response to Toys." *Infant Behavior and Development,* 1986, *9,* 257–269.

Leslie, A. M. "Pretense and Representation: The Origins of 'Theory of Mind.'" *Psychological Review,* 1987, *94,* 412–426.

Leslie, A. M. "Some Implications of Pretense for Mechanisms Underlying the Child's Theory of Mind." In J. Astington, P. Harris, and D. Olson (eds.), *Developing Theories of Mind.* Cambridge, England: Cambridge University Press, 1988.

Lewis, V., and Boucher, J. "Spontaneous, Instructed, and Elicited Play in Relatively Able Autistic Children." *British Journal of Developmental Psychology,* 1988, *6,* 325–339.

McDonald, M. A., Sigman, M. D., and Ungerer, J. A. "Intelligence and Behavior Problems in Five-Year-Olds in Relation to Representational Abilities in the Second Year of Life." *Journal of Developmental and Behavioral Pediatrics,* 1989, *10,* 86–91.

MacTurk, R. H., and others. "The Organization of Exploratory Behavior in Down Syndrome and Nondelayed Infants." *Child Development*, 1985, *56*, 573–581.

Morgan, G. A., Maslin-Cole, C. A., Biringin, Z., and Harmon, R. J. "Play Assessment of Mastery Motivation in Infants and Young Children." In C. Schaefer, K. Gitlin, and A. Sundgrund (eds.), *Play Diagnosis and Assessment*. New York: Wiley, 1991.

Motti, F., Cicchetti, D., and Sroufe, R. A. "Infant Affect Expression to Symbolic Play: The Coherence of Development in Down Syndrome Children." *Child Development*, 1983, *54*, 1168–1175.

Mundy, P., Sigman, M. D., Ungerer, J. A., and Sherman, T. "Defining the Social Deficits in Autism: The Contribution of Non-Verbal Communication Measures." *Journal of Child Psychology and Psychiatry and Allied Disciplines*, 1986, *27*, 657–669.

Perner, J. *Understanding the Representational Mind*. Cambridge, Mass.: MIT Press, 1991.

Riquet, C. B., Taylor, N. D., Benroya, S., and Klein, L. S. "Symbolic Play in Autistic, Down's, and Normal Children of Equivalent Mental Age." *Journal of Autism and Developmental Disorders*, 1981, *11*, 439–448.

Ruff, H. A. "The Measurement of Attention in High-Risk Infants." In P. M. Vietze and H. G. Vaughan (eds.), *Early Identification of Infants with Developmental Disabilities*. Philadelphia: Grune & Stratton, 1988.

Ruff, H. A., Lawson, K. R., Parrinello, R., and Weissberg, R. "Long-Term Stability of Individual Differences in Sustained Attention in the Early Years." *Child Development*, 1990, *61*, 60–76.

Ruskin, E., Mundy, P., Kasari, C., and Sigman, M. D. "Mastery Motivation in Children with Down Syndrome." Unpublished manuscript, University of California, Los Angeles, 1992.

Sigman, M. D. "Early Development of Preterm and Full-Term Infants: Exploratory Behavior in Eight-Month-Olds." *Child Development*, 1976, *47*, 606–612.

Sigman, M. D. "What Are the Core Deficits in Autism?" In S. H. Broman and J. Graffman (eds.), *Atypical Cognitive Deficits in Developmental Disorders: Implications for Brain Function*. Hillsdale, N.J.: Erlbaum, in press.

Sigman, M. D., McDonald, M. A., Neumann, C., and Bwibo, N. "Prediction of Cognitive Competence in Kenyan Children from Toddler Nutrition, Family Characteristics, and Abilities." *Journal of Child Psychology and Psychiatry and Allied Disciplines*, 1991, *32*, 307–320.

Sigman, M. D., Mundy, P., Sherman, T., and Ungerer, J. A. "Social Interactions of Autistic, Mentally Retarded, and Normal Children with Their Caregivers." *Journal of Child Psychology and Psychiatry and Allied Disciplines*, 1986, *27*, 647–656.

Sigman, M. D., and Ungerer, J. A. "Cognitive and Language Skills in Autistic, Mentally Retarded, and Normal Children." *Developmental Psychology*, 1984, *20*, 293–302.

Sigman, M. D., and others. "Home Interactions and the Development of Embu Toddlers in Kenya." *Child Development*, 1988, *59*, 1251–1261.

Sigman, M. D., and others. "Relations Between Nutrition and Development of Kenyan Toddlers." *Journal of Pediatrics*, 1989, *115*, 357–364.

Tamis-LeMonda, C. S., and Bornstein, M. H. "Habituation and Maternal Encouragement of Attention in Infancy as Predictors of Toddler Language, Play, and Representational Competence." *Child Development*, 1989, *60*, 738–751.

Tamis-LeMonda, C. S., and Bornstein, M. H. "Language, Play, and Attention at One Year." *Infant Behavior and Development*, 1990, *13*, 85–98.

Tamis-LeMonda, C. S., and Bornstein, M. H. *Representation in the Second Year: Models of Predictive Validity of Language and Play*. Unpublished manuscript, New York University and National Institute of Child Health and Human Development, 1992.

Tilton, J. R., and Ottinger, D. R. "Comparison of Toy Play Behavior of Autistic, Retarded, and Normal Children." *Psychological Report*, 1964, *15*, 967–975.

Ungerer, J. A., and Sigman, M. D. "Developmental Lags in Preterm Infants from 1 to 3 Years of Age." *Child Development*, 1983, *54*, 1217–1228.

Ungerer, J. A., and Sigman, M. D. "The Relation of Play and Sensorimotor Behavior to Language in the Second Year." *Child Development,* 1984, *55,* 1440–1455.

Vietze, P. M., and others. "Attention and Exploratory Behavior in Infants with Down's Syndrome." In T. Field and A. Sostek (eds.), *Infants Born at Risk: Physiological, Perceptual, and Cognitive Processes.* Philadelphia: Grune & Stratton, 1983.

Weiner, B., Ottinger, D., and Tilton, J. "Comparison of the Toy Play Behavior of Autistic, Retarded, and Normal Children." *Psychological Reports,* 1969, *25,* 223–227.

Weiss, B., Beeghly, M., and Cicchetti, D. "Symbolic Play Development in Children with Down Syndrome and Nonhandicapped Children." Paper presented at the biennial meeting of the Society for Research in Child Development, Toronto, Canada, April 1985.

Wing, L., Gould, L., Yeates, S. R., and Brierly, L. M. "Symbolic Play in Severely Mentally Retarded and Autistic Children." *Journal of Child Psychology and Psychiatry and Allied Disciplines,* 1977, *18,* 167–178.

MARIAN SIGMAN *is professor of psychiatry and psychology, University of California, Los Angeles.*

RHONDA SENA *is assistant professor of psychiatry, University of California, Los Angeles.*

Variability in children's play and exploration is related to a system of covarying influences, encompassing biological, experiential, and individual characteristics.

Multidimensional Correlates of Individual Variability in Play and Exploration

Theodore D. Wachs

Exploration and play are behaviors that appear in the repertoires of the overwhelming majority of mammalian species (Weisler and McCall, 1976). Even in cultures where young children are expected to assume adult work responsibilities, available literature is replete with examples of how these children manage to integrate play activities into their daily work tasks (Schwartzman, 1986). The universality of play and exploration may be functional in nature in the sense that these behaviors provide the means through which the young organism learns about its environment (Piaget, [1936] 1977), learns how to modify the environment (Garvey, 1974), and practices skills that may be important for later behavior (Bruner, 1973).

Although play may be an almost universal mammalian characteristic, this does not mean that individual variability in play can best be understood with reference to genetic "hard wiring." The capacity for play may well be genetic in nature, but interindividual variability in the extent and quality of play behavior is the rule and not the exception. An understanding of which factors are related to interindividual variability in the nature or amount of play is the key concern.

The Egyptian study of correlates of functional competence referred to in this chapter was supported by the U.S. Agency for International Development contracts DAN1309-55-1070-00 and DAN1309-A009090. Thanks go to my colleagues in this large multidisciplinary project: Zeinab Bishry, Osman Galal, Gail Harrison, Norge Jerome, Nell Kirksey, George McCabe, Farouk Shaheen, and Feisal Yunis. Special thanks to Terri Combs for her detailed work on data analysis.

What does this question have to do with understanding the role of play in the development of thought? Many of the classes of determinants that influence variability in play behavior may also be relevant to variability in the development of thought. This focus on common determinants as the link between play and thought is different from most developmental approaches, which look for direct links between play variability and variability in cognition (Athey, 1984), without considering the possibility that these links may be mediated by common determinants (Bradley, 1986).

In terms of factors that predict variability in children's play behavior, two major areas of investigation have involved the nature of the object that the child is utilizing in play (complexity and novelty; Ellis, 1984; Rubin, Fein, and Vandenberg, 1983) and the social-physical context within which the child is playing (solitary versus social play or outdoor versus indoor play; Henderson, 1984; Rubin, Fein, and Vandenberg, 1983). These factors clearly influence the nature and extent of children's ongoing play behavior, but their impact is likely to be relatively short-term in nature. My concern is for those factors that are more likely to have long-term influences on variability in play behaviors. Studies of this type usually are focused on single factors investigated in isolation (Wachs, in press). My aim in this chapter is to demonstrate the importance of focusing on systems of multiple factors considered in combination, rather than in isolation. The factors to be considered encompass environmental, biological, and individual differences domains.

Environmental Correlates

Previous infrahuman studies on the exploratory behavior of animals reared in isolation (Menzel, Davenport, and Rogers, 1963; Sackett, 1972) and human studies on infants reared in institutions (Collard, 1971; Rheingold, 1961) provide valuable demonstrations of the relevance of environment to variability in exploration and play. However, these types of studies tell us little about which specific dimensions of the environment are salient. Recent studies have identified specific environmental dimensions that relate to variability in children's play behaviors:

1. *Caregiver mediation* of the child's play behavior with objects, which is positively related to higher levels of exploration and play (Belsky, 1980; Belsky, Goode, and Most, 1980; Cohen and Tomlinson-Keasey, 1980; Landry, Chapieski, and Schmidt, 1986; Teti, Bond, and Gibbs, 1988; Wachs, 1987; Yarrow and others, 1984).

2. *Caregiver verbal stimulation,* which is positively associated with the level and extent of exploratory and play behavior (Belsky, 1980; Slade, 1987; Wachs, 1987; Yarrow and others, 1982).

3. *Caregiver restrictions* of the child's exploratory or play behavior,

which are found to inhibit subsequent exploration or play (Belsky, 1980; Howes and Stewart, 1987; Jennings and others, 1979; Power, 1985; Rubenstein and Howes, 1979; Slade, 1987).

4. *Caregiver positive affect* during play, which is positively related to subsequent level or extent of exploration and play (Jennings and Connor, 1989; Rubenstein and Howes, 1979; Spangler, 1989).

5. *Other dimensions of caregiver behavior* that have been tentatively identified as relevant to play variability include sensory stimulation (Yarrow and others, 1982), caregiver sensitivity (Frodi, Bridges, and Grolnick, 1985), and caregiver involvement (Spangler, 1989).

6. The quality of the child's *physical environment* has also been implicated in variability in exploration and play competence. Relevant dimensions include object availability and variety (McQuiston and Wachs, 1979; Yarrow, Rubenstein, and Pedersen, 1975), the presence of audiovisually responsive toys in the home (Jennings and others, 1979), and homes characterized by low levels of crowding (McQuiston and Wachs, 1979; Udwin and Shmukler, 1981; Wachs, 1987).

All of the studies cited above utilized children in Western developed countries as subjects. However, there is recent evidence that a number of the environmental dimensions cited above (verbal stimulation, parental involvement, and crowding) show the same pattern of relations to the behavior of children in non-Western, less developed countries (Wachs and others, in press *b*).

A Study of Multidimensional Correlates in Another Culture. There is ample evidence relating environment to variability in play behaviors, but it may be a mistake to consider the relation of environment to play in isolation. To document this point, I use data from a large, longitudinal study conducted in Egypt on the effects of nutritional intake and its covariates on children's functional competence.

The performance site for this study was the village of Kalama, Egypt. Kalama has a population over eight thousand and is located in the Nile Delta, twenty-five kilometers north of downtown Cairo. Our sample consisted of 153 toddlers (77 males, 76 females) and their caregivers. Toddlers entered the study at seventeen months of age and exited it at thirty months of age. Even by Egyptian standards our subject population was skewed toward a lower demographic group, with 79 percent of our sample rated as low socioeconomic status (laborers and farm hands).

Between eighteen and thirty months of age all toddlers were observed twice a month for thirty minutes per observation period, using naturalistic observational procedures. Observational measures included twelve codes characterizing the quality of the child's psychosocial rearing environment (caregiver availability, vocal stimulation of the child, physical contact stimulation, and caregiver responsivity). Among the child behavioral data obtained during our observations was a measure of the child's exploration and play, namely, the degree of the child's involvement with persons and objects in his or her environment.

Over the same age period, trained dieticians independently collected measures of toddler dietary intake, using a combination of probed oral recall and weighing of food portions. Nutritional content of food consumed was determined through use of food composition tables and laboratory analyses of indigenous foods. Although not malnourished, our toddlers were classified as having intakes below recommended daily allowances.

During the same age period, project physicians visited homes weekly to assess degree and type of child illness. At twenty-four and thirty months, Egyptian psychologists tested toddlers on a developmental battery, which included a measure of play competence. Specifically, toddlers were allowed ten minutes to play with a set of ten culturally familiar toys. Psychologists coded the types of play behaviors exhibited by the toddlers. Our toy-play codes were derived from those developed by Ungerer and Sigman (1984) and included measures of (1) *exploration,* visually attending to an object while manipulating the object in an exploratory manner (for example, turning the object around or feeling the object's surface); (2) *relational play,* combining two or more objects in ways not typically associated with the objects' design functions (for example, banging two objects together or placing one object inside another); (3) *functional play,* using objects together in ways typically associated with the objects' design functions, whether involving two objects (for example, placing a spoon inside a cup or brushing a doll's hair with a brush) or an object and a person (for example, the child brushing his or her own hair with a brush); (4) *symbolic play,* using abstracting capacities such as substitution play, where one object is used as if it were another (for example, using a tea cup as a telephone receiver), or imaginary play, where nonexistent objects are invoked (for example, making pouring sounds and saying "tea" as the child pretends to hold a tea pot in one hand and a cup in another); and (5) *social play,* attempting to get the adult involved in the ongoing play (for example, standing next to an adult and holding an object out to the adult while looking at the adult).

Multiple Correlates: Morbidity, Environment, and Play. In developed countries, most mild, nonchronic child illnesses appear to have few long-term consequences for children's development; high levels of childhood morbidity may have more serious developmental consequences for children in less developed countries (Pollitt, 1983). Inspection of the impact of childhood morbidity in our Egyptian population revealed that morbidity covaries *both* with toddler play and with caregiver behavioral patterns toward the toddler. Toddlers in this study were not observed or tested when they were acutely ill. Specifically, the percentage of days that children were ill with fever was negatively related to both the degree of toddler-adult interaction ($r = -.20$, $p < .05$) and the degree of the toddlers' simultaneous interaction with both persons and objects in their environments ($r = -.18$, $p < .05$), as well as with lower caregiver vocal stimulation ($r = -.28$, $p < .01$). The percentage of days that children were ill with gastrointestinal disorders was negatively related to the degree of toddler person-object interaction ($r = -.32$, $p < .01$) and with caregiver vocal stimulation ($r = -.30$, $p < .01$) but positively associated with less responsivity to toddler vocalizations ($r = .25$, $p < .01$) and distress ($r = .20$, $p < .05$). The addition of morbidity into this analysis of environment-involvement relations resulted in an increment of nearly 6 percent of unique predictive variance (Wachs and others, in press b).

These results suggest that in less developed countries the context of the young child encompasses the covariance between rearing environment and child morbidity. Better prediction of variability in child play occurs when the contributions of these covariates are integrated rather than treated in isolation. This integration is particularly important for understanding variability in children's play in cultures other than our own.

Biological Correlates

A consistent theme in the human nutrition literature is the reduction in the level and quality of children's exploration or play as a consequence of moderate to severe malnutrition (Barrett and Radke-Yarrow, 1985; Chavez and Martinez, 1984; Grantham-McGregor, 1984). What is not clear is which specific nutrients relate to variability in children's exploration or play. This lack of clarity is particularly evident for children who are chronically undernourished but not malnourished.

Nutrition and Play. Two parallel studies carried out in Egypt and Kenya have recently shed light on the question of which nutrients relate to variability in children's play. Although there are clear differences between these two countries in terms of both the level of intake and the nature of specific nutrients consumed, there were two common findings across projects. First, in both Egypt and Kenya, the component of play most strongly related to nutrition was *symbolic play*. Second, level of *protein intake* related to the degree of toddlers' symbolic play behavior (Sigman and others, 1989; Wachs and others, in press a).

One explanation for these findings is that it is not so much protein intake per se as the intake of specific micronutrients such as iron (which are associated with protein intake) that relates to play (Pollitt, Lewis, Leibel, and Greenfield, 1981). To test the question of whether nutritional influences on symbolic play behavior relate to micro- as well as macronutrients, we regressed thirteen micronutrients onto toddler symbolic play behavior. As summarized in Table 4.1, we were able to identify three vitamins (vitamin A, vitamin A from animal sources, vitamin B_{12}) and one trace mineral (calcium) that add unique predictive variance to variability in symbolic play, even when all other micronutrients are partialed out. What is common to all four of these micronutrients is that they derive from intake of *animal source* foods. In both Egypt and Kenya there is converging data that implicate animal source intake as a key nutritional factor related to variability in cognitive development. Clearly, there is a parallel between nutritional influences that are related to cognitive development and those that are related to a cognitively loaded aspect of children's play behavior, namely, symbolic play.

Multiple Correlates: Nutrition, Environment, and Play. In both Egypt and Kenya the quality of the toddler's nutritional intake covaries with the quality of the toddler's psychosocial rearing environment (Wachs and others, 1992). The implications of this covariance are seen when we consider the interaction between macronutrient intake and either of two measures of the quality of the toddler's psychosocial rearing environment: (inappropriate) nonverbal responsivity to the child's vocalization and caregiver vocal stimulation. Specifically, a significant increment in our ability to predict toddler symbolic play occurs when we move from intake of calories from animal sources considered in isolation ($R^2 = .097$) either to the combination of animal source calories and nonverbal responsivity ($R^2 = .220$; significance of change, $F = 3.46$, $p < .05$) or to the combination of animal source calories and vocal stimulation ($R^2 = .274$; significance of change, $F = 5.35$, $p < .05$) (Wachs and others, in press *a*). This

Table 4.1. Unique Contribution of Select Micronutrients to Symbolic Play

Micronutrients	Percentage Unique Variance	F
Vitamin C	0.00	0.00
Thiamin	0.07	1.12
Riboflavin	0.00	0.14
Niacin	1.04	1.54
Vitamin B_6	0.00	0.67
Vitamin B_{12}	5.64	8.30[b]
Animal source vitamin A	3.24	4.77[a]
Vitamin A	3.88	5.72[a]
Iron	1.85	2.73
Zinc	0.00	0.61
Calcium	5.90	8.69[b]
Vitamin D	1.44	2.13
Folate	1.52	2.25

Note: Overall R^2 between micronutrients and play = .66 ($p < .01$).

[a] $p < .05$

[b] $p < .01$

evidence further illustrates the importance of looking at variability in play behavior as a function of the operation of a system of interrelated influences.

Individual Differences Correlates

Variability in play behavior is also related to variability in individual characteristics. Studies of individual differences correlates of variability in children's play behavior, such as sex differences (Rubin, Fein, and Vandenberg, 1983) or developmental disabilities (Quinn and Rubin, 1984), have looked at individual differences in isolation. However, evidence exists supporting the proposition that a multidimensional approach may be more appropriate. Results from two studies converge on an interaction between individual characteristics and environmental stimuli as these relate to toddlers' play behavior. Specifically, these studies indicate that infants who are characterized as *highly active* show higher levels of mastery play (Wachs, 1987) and exploratory play competence (Gandour, 1989) when their parents are *less stimulating* or less involved; the reverse pattern holds for low-active infants. If there are interactions between individual and environmental characteristics, the critical question is, Which individual and environmental characteristics are most likely to interact? One highly speculative answer, with potential relevance for play and thought, is described below.

Across a number of domains, a distinction has been made between children whose development is characterized primarily by a focus on objects and children whose development is characterized primarily by a focus on persons. This dichotomy appears in such diverse areas as early language development (Nelson, 1981), classroom behavior (Nakamura and Finck, 1980), reactivity to institutional environments (Langmeier and Matejcek, 1975), attentional patterns (Escalona, 1968; Parrinello and Ruff, 1988), and temperament (Balleyguier, 1991). Shotwell, Wolf, and Gardner (1980) identified this person-object dichotomy when looking at differences in children's symbolic play styles. However, their data are based on a small sample of children ($N = 9$) and on only one specific domain of play (symbolic).

How generalizable is this dichotomy to other areas of children's play? To answer this question, we conducted a cluster analysis (Ward's minimum variance method) of the mastery play of sixty-four twelve-month-old children (Wachs and Combs, in press). Four of our play codes assessed the infant's behavior toward objects when the infant was ignoring the examiner; two codes assessed the infant's attempt to play with the adult while ignoring objects; the final code assessed the degree to which the infant attempted to involve the adult in object play. Our analysis showed that one cluster was composed of children with relatively high levels of object exploration and object mastery play and relatively low levels of social mastery play and social orientation (55 percent of our sample). Toddlers in this cluster clearly fit the description of the object-oriented child. The second cluster was composed of children with low levels of object mastery play and with relatively high levels of social mastery play, passive social orientation, and joint adult-object play (45 percent of sample). This cluster seems to define children who are primarily person-oriented in nature. These results support the person-object play dichotomy among children first demonstrated by Shotwell, Wolf, and Gardner (1980), but with a larger sample and a different set of play criteria.

What are the implications of this dichotomy for understanding children's play behavior? A number of studies have noted individual differences in the extent to which caregivers emphasize social or object play with their young children (Fagot, 1978; Vibbert and Bornstein, 1989). These individual differences in infant characteristics and caregiver styles suggest the possibility of viewing variability in children's object versus social play not so much as a main-effect phenomenon ascribable either to infant characteristics or to caregiver styles but rather as a function of the degree of *fit* between child characteristics and caregiver style. That is, we should expect higher-level play behavior when object-oriented children have caregivers who are also object-oriented, and when socially oriented children have caregivers who are also socially oriented (positive fit). Less adequate play behavior should occur when object-oriented children encounter socially oriented caregivers, and vice versa (negative fit).

The implications of this fit model go beyond the development of play style per se. Given that play is seen as a major mechanism through which children learn about their environment (Rubin, Fein, and Vandenberg, 1983), I contend that a positive fit between children's and caregivers' social or object orientation should result not only in higher levels of play but also in higher levels of problem-solving skills. Similarly, a negative fit should be associated not only with decrements in play behavior but also with lower levels of cognitive and problem-solving performance. The critical point is that it is not the individual's characteristics or the caregiver's style that is associated with individual variability but rather the degree of fit between child and caregiver characteristics.

Conclusion

There is ample evidence of linkages between the development of play and the development of children's cognitive functioning (Rubin, Fein, and Vandenberg, 1983). The processes underlying these linkages are less clear. One argument of this chapter is that the same factors that underlie variability in children's play behavior may also underlie variability in children's cognitive development. A second, more critical argument is that it is not sufficient to study the operation of these underlying "determinants" in isolation. Variability in children's development is related to a multidimensional system, encompassing biological, psychosocial, and individual characteristics. These factors covary and interact with one another. It is through this process of covariance and interaction that variability in development occurs. If we are to understand the nature of the linkages between play and thought, it is essential that our research investigations mirror the nature of this multidimensional process.

References

Athey, I. "Contributions of Play to Development." In T. Yawkey and A. Pellegrini (eds.), *Child's Play: Developmental and Applied*. Hillsdale, N.J.: Erlbaum, 1984.

Balleyguier, G. "The Structure of Infant Personality and Its Comparison with the Big 5 Model." Paper presented at the conference "Development of the Structure of Temperament and Personality from Infancy to Adulthood," Wassenaar, The Netherlands, June 1991.

Barrett, D., and Radke-Yarrow, M. "Effects of Nutritional Supplementation on Children's Responses to Novel, Frustrating, and Competitive Situations." *American Journal of Clinical Nutrition*, 1985, *42*, 102–120.

Belsky, J. "A Familial Analysis of Parental Influences on Infant Exploratory Competence." In F. Pedersen (ed.), *The Father-Infant Relationship*. New York: Praeger, 1980.

Belsky, J., Goode, M. K., and Most, R. K. "Maternal Stimulation and Infant Exploratory Competence: Cross-Sectional, Correlational, and Experimental Analyses." *Child Development*, 1980, *51*, 1168–1178.

Bradley, R. "Play Materials and Intellectual Development." In A. Gottfried and C. Brown (eds.), *Play Interactions*. Lexington, Mass.: Heath, 1986.

Bruner, J. "Organization of Early Skilled Action." *Child Development*, 1973, *44*, 1–11.

Chavez, A., and Martinez, C. "Behavioral Measurements of Activity in Children and Their Relation to Food Intake in a Poor Community." In E. Pollitt and P. Amante (eds.), *Energy Intake and Activity*. New York: Liss, 1984.

Cohen, N., and Tomlinson-Keasey, C. "The Effects of Peers and Mothers on Toddler's Play." *Child Development*, 1980, *51*, 921–924.

Collard, R. "Exploratory and Play Behaviors of Infants Reared in an Institution and in Lower- and Middle-Class Homes." *Child Development*, 1971, *42*, 1003–1015.

Ellis, M. "Play, Novelty, and Stimulus Seeking." In T. Yawkey and A. Pellegrini (eds.), *Child's Play: Developmental and Applied*. Hillsdale, N.J.: Erlbaum, 1984.

Escalona, S. *The Roots of Individuality*. Hawthorne, N.Y.: Aldine, 1968.

Fagot, B. "The Influence of Sex of Child on Parental Reactions to Toddlers." *Child Development*, 1978, *49*, 459–465.

Frodi, A., Bridges, L., and Grolnick, W. "Correlates of Mastery Related Behavior." *Child Development*, 1985, *56*, 1291–1298.

Gandour, M. "Activity Level as a Dimension of Temperament in Toddlers: Its Relevance for the Organismic Specificity Hypothesis." *Child Development*, 1989, *60*, 1092–1098.

Garvey, C. "Some Properties of Social Play." *Merrill-Palmer Quarterly*, 1974, *20*, 163–180.

Grantham-McGregor, S. "Chronic Undernutrition and Cognitive Abilities." *Human Nutrition: Clinical Nutrition*, 1984, *38*, 83–94.

Henderson, B. "The Social Context of Exploratory Play." In T. Yawkey and A. Pellegrini (eds.), *Child's Play: Developmental and Applied*. Hillsdale, N.J.: Erlbaum, 1984.

Howes, C., and Stewart, P. "Child's Play with Adults, Toys, and Peers: An Examination of Family and Child-Care Influences." *Developmental Psychology*, 1987, *23*, 423–430.

Jennings, K. D., and Connors, R. E. "Mothers' Interactional Style and Children's Competence at 3 Years." *International Journal of Behavioral Development,* 1989, *12,* 155–175.

Jennings, K. D., and others. "Exploratory Play as an Index of Mastery Motivation: Relationships to Persistence, Cognitive Functioning, and Environmental Measures." *Developmental Psychology,* 1979, *15,* 386–394.

Landry, S. H., Chapieski, M. L., and Schmidt, M. "Effects of Maternal Attention Directing Strategies on Preterms' Response to Toys." *Infant Behavior and Development,* 1986, *9,* 257–269.

Langmeier, J., and Matejcek, Z. *Psychological Deprivation in Childhood.* New York: Wiley, 1975.

McQuiston, S., and Wachs, T. D. "Developmental Changes in the Nature of Infants' Exploratory Behavior." Paper presented at the biennial meeting of the Society for Research in Child Development, San Francisco, March 1979.

Menzel, E., Davenport, R., and Rogers, C. "The Effects of Environmental Restriction upon Chimpanzees' Responsiveness to Objects." *Journal of Comparative and Physiological Psychology,* 1963, *56,* 78–85.

Nakamura, C., and Finck, D. *Relative Effectiveness of Socially Oriented and Task-Oriented Children and Predictability of Their Behaviors.* Monographs of the Society for Research in Child Development, vol. 45, nos. 3–4 (serial no. 185). Chicago: University of Chicago Press, 1980.

Nelson, K. "Individual Differences in Language Development." *Developmental Psychology,* 1981, *17,* 170–187.

Parrinello, R., and Ruff, H. A. "The Influence of Adult Intervention and Infants' Level of Attention." *Child Development,* 1988, *59,* 1125–1135.

Piaget, J. "The Origins of Intelligence in Children." In H. Gruber and V. Voneche (eds.), *The Essential Piaget.* New York: Basic Books, 1977. (Originally published 1936.)

Pollitt, E. "Morbidity and Infant Development: An Hypothesis." *International Journal of Behavioral Development,* 1983, *6,* 461–467.

Pollitt, E., Lewis, M., Leibel, R., and Greenfield, D. "Iron Deficiency and Play Behavior in Preschool Children." In P. Garry (ed.), *Human Nutrition: Clinical and Biochemical Aspects.* Washington, D.C.: American Association of Clinical Chemistry, 1981.

Power, T. G. "Mother- and Father-Infant Play: A Developmental Analysis." *Child Development,* 1985, *56,* 1514–1524.

Quinn, J., and Rubin, K. "The Play of Handicapped Children." In T. Yawkey and A. Pellegrini (eds.), *Child's Play: Developmental and Applied.* Hillsdale, N.J.: Erlbaum, 1984.

Rheingold, H. "The Effect of Environmental Stimulation upon Social and Exploratory Behavior of the Infant." In B. Foss (ed.), *Determinants of Infant Behavior.* London: Methuen, 1961.

Rubenstein, J., and Howes, C. "Caregiving and Infant Behavior in Daycare and in Homes." *Developmental Psychology,* 1979, *15,* 1–24.

Rubin, K., Fein, G., and Vandenberg, B. "Play." In M. Hetherington (ed.), *Handbook of Child Psychology.* Vol. 4: *Socialization, Personality, and Social Development.* New York: Wiley, 1983.

Sackett, G. "Exploratory Behavior of Rhesus Monkeys as a Function of Rearing Experiences and Sex." *Developmental Psychology,* 1972, *6,* 260–270.

Schwartzman, H. "A Cross-Cultural Perspective on Child-Structured Play Activities and Material." In A. Gottfried and C. Brown (eds.), *Play Interactions.* Lexington, Mass.: Heath, 1986.

Shotwell, J., Wolf, D., and Gardner, H. "Styles of Achievement in Early Symbol Use." In M. Foster and S. Brandes (eds.), *Symbol as Sense.* San Diego: Academic Press, 1980.

Sigman, M. D., and others. "Relationship Between Nutrition and Development in Kenyan Toddlers." *Journal of Pediatrics,* 1989, *115,* 357–364.

Slade, A. "A Longitudinal Study of Maternal Involvement and Symbolic Play During the Toddler Period." *Child Development*, 1987, *58*, 367–375.

Spangler, G. "Toddlers' Everyday Experiences as Related to Preceding Mental and Emotional Disposition and Their Relationship to Subsequent Mental and Motivational Development: A Short-Term Longitudinal Study." *International Journal of Behavioral Development*, 1989, *12*, 285–303.

Teti, D., Bond, L., and Gibbs, E. "Mothers, Fathers, and Siblings: A Comparison of Play Styles and Their Influence upon Infant Cognitive Development." *International Journal of Behavioral Development*, 1988, *11*, 415–432.

Udwin, O., and Shmukler, D. "The Influence of Sociocultural, Economic, and Home Background Factors on Children's Ability to Engage in Imaginative Play." *Developmental Psychology*, 1981, *17*, 66–72.

Ungerer, J. A., and Sigman, M. D. "The Relation of Play and Sensorimotor Behavior to Language in the Second Year." *Child Development*, 1984, *55*, 1440–1455.

Vibbert, M., and Bornstein, M. H. "Specific Associations Between Domains of Mother-Child Interaction and Toddler Referential Language and Pretense Play." *Infant Behavior and Development*, 1989, *12*, 163–184.

Wachs, T. D. "Specificity of Environmental Action as Manifest in Environmental Correlates of Infant's Mastery Motivation." *Developmental Psychology*, 1987, *23*, 782–790.

Wachs, T. D. "Determinants of Intellectual Development: Single Determinant Research in a Multideterminant Universe." *Intelligence*, in press.

Wachs, T. D., and Combs, T. "The Domains of Mastery Motivation." In R. H. MacTurk and G. Morgan (eds.), *Mastery Motivation: Conceptual Origins and Applications*. Norwood, N.J.: Ablex, in press.

Wachs, T. D., and others. "Caregiver Child Interaction Patterns in Two Cultures in Relation to Nutrition." *International Journal of Behavioral Development*, 1992, *15*, 1–18.

Wachs, T. D., and others. "Relations Between Nutrition and Cognitive Performance in Egyptian Toddlers." *Intelligence*, in press a.

Wachs, T. D., and others. "Relation of Rearing Environment to Adaptive Behavior of Egyptian Toddlers." *Child Development*, in press b.

Weisler, A., and McCall, R. "Exploration and Play." *American Psychologist*, 1976, *31*, 492–508.

Yarrow, L., Rubenstein, J., and Pedersen, F. *Infant and Environment*. New York: Wiley, 1975.

Yarrow, L., and others. "Infants' Persistence on Tasks: Relationships to Cognitive Functioning and Early Experience." *Infant Behavior and Development*, 1982, *5*, 131–141.

Yarrow, L., and others. "The Developmental Course of Parental Stimulation and Its Relationship to Mastery Motivation During Infancy." *Developmental Psychology*, 1984, *20*, 492–503.

THEODORE D. WACHS is professor of psychological sciences, Purdue University, West Lafayette, Indiana.

*Caregiver activities during play with infants and toddlers are
explored, considering both social and didactic types of parent-child
interactions and the ways in which child play is enhanced during
interactions with a sophisticated and responsive partner.*

Caregiver-Child Interaction in Play

Anne Watson O'Reilly, Marc H. Bornstein

Two salient kinds of interactions of caregivers with children can be broadly
characterized as social and didactic (Bornstein, 1989). Social behaviors
involve reciprocity, turn taking, and expressions of affect. Didactic behaviors generally consist of direct teaching, focusing of attention, labeling, and
provision of information. In this chapter, we explore these dimensions of
caregiver-child interaction in the domain of play. Child play shows a
developmental progression across the first two years of life and also offers
the opportunity to track changes in caregiver behaviors as the child
matures. Specifically, we look at what caregivers do in play interactions
with children, and how they adjust play as children develop. We also
explore differences between child play alone and with a caregiver, and we
examine individual differences in caregiver behaviors and their relation to
individual differences in child play. The extent and limits of our current
understanding of child play are evaluated as this review lays the groundwork for future research concerning the influence of parental behaviors on
mental growth in children, using child play as one measure of cognitive
ability, and the social and didactic behaviors within and outside of play for
assessing parental contributions.

Caregiver-Child Interaction in Play

Much of caregiver-infant interaction in the home occurs in situations other
than play, and much of child play in the first years of life is actually solitary
(Carew, 1980; Dunn and Wooding, 1977; Green, Gustafson, and West,
1980). However, parents commonly structure the context of their children's
play to allow access to adult interaction and guidance (Bradley and Cald-

well, 1984; Wachs, 1984). For example, Dunn and Wooding (1977) observed naturalistic play of eighteen- to twenty-four-month-olds in the home; children initiated the majority of pretend play sequences but completed them with the help of the mother. Likewise, Klein (1988) found that over the course of the first two years, parents changed in their choice of context for "mediated learning experiences"—situations in which the environment is interpreted and structured for the child in a developmentally appropriate manner—increasingly seeing play as a proper situation for adult-guided learning.

There is preliminary evidence of an important role for caregiver social and didactic behaviors in play. When parents are actively engaged in play with their children, they structure play by providing props, guide by helping children maintain roles and the action, establish and arrange the play context, engage in play as a partner, and monitor play and give feedback (Göncü, 1987; Miller and Garvey, 1984; Sachs, 1980). Göncü (1987) has labeled these adult behaviors the "director," "co-player," and "spectator" roles. In addition, parents show their children that play can be "enjoyable" (Sachs, 1980).

Changes in Child Play and in Caregiver Play with Child Development

Starting in the middle of their first year, infants actively explore objects, initially mouthing and then manipulating them. Toward the end of the first year, they begin to act on the functions of objects and functional relations between objects. Over the course of the second year, toddlers achieve the ability to perform symbolic actions with objects, from simple pretense behaviors directed toward the self to more sophisticated forms of pretense involving planned sequences of pretend actions and object substitutions (Belsky and Most, 1981; Fenson and Ramsey, 1980; Nicolich, 1977; Ruff, 1984; Ungerer, Zelazo, Kearsley, and O'Leary, 1981). Play has therefore been viewed as one form of the child's growing *representational competence* or capacity for symbolic thought. Another such form is language, and there is empirical evidence that play and language are related in young children, suggesting that both are rooted in the acquisition of a symbol system (Bornstein, Vibbert, Tal, and O'Donnell, 1992; Bretherton and Bates, 1984; McCune-Nicolich, 1981; Tamis-LeMonda and Bornstein, 1989, 1990, this volume; Ungerer and Sigman, 1984; Vibbert and Bornstein, 1989; Werner and Kaplan, 1963).

These changes in child play ability are matched by changes in parental play. For example, in a cross-sectional study of play, Rogoff, Malkin, and Gilbride (1984) found that the focus of free play at four months was joint attention, between five and twelve months it was joint play with toys, and between twelve and seventeen months it was maintenance of the play relationship through symbolic messages. Further, Tamis-LeMonda and Bornstein (1991) reported that features of mother and child play correspond at thirteen and twenty months and that the sophistication of mother and child play changes from the younger to the older age. Increasingly across the second and third years, parents use words to regulate play activity between a child and adult (Dixon and Shore, 1990; Eckerman and Didow, 1989; O'Connell and Bretherton, 1984). Sachs (1980, 1984) observed a shift in preponderance of speech type of parents—from suggestions in play ("feed the dolly") to descriptions ("the dolly's crying"), which matched a developmental shift in child play toward attributing animate characteristics to dolls. At the younger age range, adults often supply the narrative thread in play.

Thus, adults show sensitivity to developmental changes in their children's play, particularly with respect to their use of language in the play context. As children become more competent players, adults shift their behaviors during play to more sophisticated levels. There may be limits to parental sensitivity, however. O'Connell and Bretherton (1984) found that from twenty to twenty-eight months there were no differences in the frequency or distribution of maternal play prompts with children. Mothers provided a wide range of suggestions and made many more suggestions than their children could possibly follow. However, at twenty-eight months, the children responded more frequently to suggestions for symbolic play than at twenty months, indicating that children differentially select from their mothers' behaviors those that they are capable of comprehending and acting on at a particular stage in development. Goodwyn, Acredolo, and Fulmer (1992) similarly concluded that factors within children often determine the effectiveness of maternal input. They argue that the later emergence of a positive relation between maternal play and vocabulary growth for boys as compared to girls, given no difference at any age in maternal play by child sex, is based on a sex difference in language maturation.

Child Play Alone Versus Child Play with a Caregiver

In order to explore relations between parental behaviors and child play in greater depth, we distinguish two types of child play with mother: prompted play and spontaneous play (O'Connell and Bretherton, 1984; Slade, 1987a; Tamis-LeMonda and Bornstein, 1991). During play with their children, mothers frequently attempt to direct child play through demonstrations and solicitations. Demonstrations and solicitations are didactic caregiver behaviors. For example, a mother might pick up a set of nesting barrels and show her child how they go together. Or a mother might hand two nesting barrels to her child and ask, "Can you put these together?" If the child responds to these demonstrations and solicitations, we call that *prompted child play with mother.* Alternatively, a child can initiate play in the presence of the mother. For example, the child might pick up a set of nesting barrels and begin nesting. We call this *spontaneous play with mother.*

Maternal participation in child play lengthens play bouts, raises the level of sophistication of those bouts, and makes child play more diverse, in comparison to solitary child play (Dunn and Wooding, 1977; Fiese, 1990; O'Connell and Bretherton, 1984; Slade, 1987a; Zukow, 1986). These findings lend support to the Vygotskian notion that during joint activity with a more sophisticated partner, children are provided the opportunity to perform at levels above those that they achieve on their own (Vygotsky, 1978; Wertsch, 1979). A finer analysis of these data indicates that the highest level of child play occurs in direct response to maternal demonstrations and solicitations: When mothers prompt child play, child play is more sophisticated than either spontaneous child play with mother or play alone (Slade, 1987a; O'Connell and Bretherton, 1984).

We can also compare spontaneous child play with mother to child play alone. Results from one study suggest that spontaneous child play with mother is not different from child play alone. O'Connell and Bretherton (1984) found that when child responses to maternal verbal and gestural directives, in addition to imitations of the mother's activities (in other words, prompted play), were removed, the diversity of child play with mother was not different from child play alone. However, the mothers in this study were explicitly instructed to show their children how to use the toys provided, and, under these conditions, spontaneous play with mother might be somewhat constrained compared to mother-child play that is less structured.

We conducted a study of caregiver-child interaction to compare child play alone with prompted and spontaneous play with mother, without giving mothers any explicit instructions about how to play. Our sample includes fifty-five mother-child dyads, each visited in the home when the child was twenty months old. Two ten-minute play sessions were videotaped: a child play-alone session and a child play-with-mother session. Our measure of play sophistication was an eight-level play scale (see Tamis-LeMonda and Bornstein, this volume, for a description of this play scale and a comparison with scales described in other chapters), adapted to a computer-based system for comprehensively coding videorecords of the behaviors of mothers and children. The eight play levels range from unitary functional activity to substitution pretense. The four lower levels can be grouped together to form a measure of nonsymbolic play, and the four upper levels can be grouped to form a measure of symbolic play.

Using a measure of average level of nonsymbolic play and a measure of average level of symbolic play, we found that spontaneous child play with mother was not different from child play alone. These measures of play are similar, although not identical, to those used by O'Connell and

Bretherton (1984). However, when considering the relative proportions of nonsymbolic and symbolic play, we found a dramatically decreased frequency of nonsymbolic play bouts in spontaneous child play with mother compared to child play alone (a difference not due to a warm-up effect). There was a significant linear trend in these data across the three situations: more nonsymbolic play occurred in play alone compared to spontaneous play with mother, which in turn involved more nonsymbolic play than prompted play with mother. Our results support those of O'Connell and Bretherton: In terms of sophistication of either nonsymbolic or symbolic play, the differences between child play alone and with mother are due to direct child responses to maternal prompts. However, there is much less nonsymbolic play with mother in spontaneous as well as prompted play compared to child play alone. This finding concurs with Dunn and Wooding's (1977) observation that, in two-year-olds' play in the home, nonsymbolic exploratory play characterizes child play alone and is rarely seen when mothers are playing with their children. It is probably the case that the social nature of symbolic play at this age, and its association with language (Bruner, 1981; Sigman, in press), decreases the likelihood that nonsymbolic exploratory activities will appear in joint play.

This finding also suggests the importance of examining social interactions when evaluating symbolic play in the dyad. Fiese (1990) found that maternal intrusions and questioning were positively associated with simple exploratory play and negatively associated with symbolic play in fifteen- to twenty-four-month-olds' play with mothers. Interactional reciprocity was likely to precede higher-level symbolic play, whereas intrusiveness, onlooking, and child initiations preceded lower-level exploratory play. These results further demonstrate the preponderance of symbolic play within the context of reciprocal social interactions.

Individual Differences in Caregiver Behaviors and Their Relation to Child Play

Fiese's (1990) unit of analysis was the child play bout, and she examined the relation between features of maternal and child behavior connected to the bout. Her finding that symbolic play is associated with particular types of maternal involvement and child behavior suggests that dyads with more of these characteristics might engage in a greater amount of symbolic play. An examination of individual differences in parental social and didactic behaviors and their relation to individual differences in child play supports the idea that the degree to which mothers guide and participate in play is related to the level of the child's play when children are playing with their mothers. For example, mothers who engage in more symbolic play have children who do more symbolic play with their mother (Unger and Howes, 1988). Tamis-LeMonda and Bornstein (1991) found significant associations between the amount and sophistication of mothers' demonstrations and solicitations of play and their children's spontaneous and prompted play with mother at twenty months. In a cross-cultural comparison, Tamis-LeMonda and others (1992) reported that U.S. mothers do more non-symbolic play with children, whereas Japanese mothers do more symbolic play (in particular, other-directed pretense). Concomitantly, play by Japanese and U.S. children matched differences in maternal play: Japanese children engage in more symbolic play.

Support for the importance of assessing individual differences in the quality of social interactions in play comes from research on special populations. Deaf children, who are at risk for delayed language acquisition and difficult social interactions, show higher levels of play ability when their interactions with mothers involve more smiling and positive facial expression (Spenser and Deyo, 1993). Tingley and Golden (1992) found qualitatively distinct processes of interaction in play between children and their well versus depressed mothers. Interaction during play was more organized in well than in depressed dyads in this study, even though the overall amount of symbolic play was found to be similar across the two groups. Finally, higher-level play was associated with positive affect and proportion of time engaged in structured social turn-taking games with mother in a sample of Down syndrome children and cognitively matched nonretarded controls (Beeghly, Perry, and Cicchetti, 1989).

There is also evidence that individual differences in caregiver behaviors outside of the play setting relate to differences in children's play sophistication. Belsky, Goode, and Most (1980) reported that the degree to which mothers focused their children's attention toward objects and events in the environment (through physical means such as pointing, showing, and demonstrating) was significantly positively correlated with exploratory competence (play) in children at twelve months of age. Vibbert and Bornstein (1989) found support for the joint association of different kinds of parental behaviors with child play. The combination of mothers' positive social interaction and didactic stimulation (observed naturalistically in the home outside of the play setting) related to their thirteen-month-olds' play sophistication as measured by a composite score of spontaneous play alone and experimenter-elicited play. Children's play was most sophisticated when there was frequent social interaction and frequent didactic encouragement of attention to the environment, independently of who took the lead in maintaining object-focused interaction. Finally, amount of verbal stimulation in the environment has been found to relate positively to child play ability in toddlers in rural Kenya (Sigman and others, 1988; Sigman, McDonald, Neumann, and Bwibo, 1991).

Families who are nurturing have children with higher levels of competent play with adult caregivers, with peers, and with toys (Howes and Stewart, 1987; Jennings and Connors, 1989). In addition, several studies suggest that security of child attachment relates positively to child play. Baruch (1991) found that maternal sensitivity and attachment security predicted sophistication of child play in a stressful (postmodeling), but not in an unstressful, play situation. Securely attached twelve- and thirteen-month-olds show less discrepancy between their elicited and free-play scores (Belsky, Garduque, and Hrncir, 1984). In a study conducted by Slade (1987b), securely attached twenty- to twenty-eight-month-olds played longer and at higher levels with their mothers than did anxiously attached children, but the two types of children did not differ in their play ability when playing alone. Thus, securely and anxiously attached children do not necessarily differ in their cognitive competence, as has been previously supposed (Matas, Arend, and Sroufe, 1978); rather, competence interacts with social context.

Parental Behavior and Child Cognitive Growth

There is a growing body of research to show that caregivers influence intellectual development and that the child's cognitive advancement is facilitated in particular by interactions that are reciprocal, warm, positive, and supportive, in contrast to controlling, intrusive, and unresponsive, within the context of instruction and joint problem solving (Clarke-Stewart, 1973; Elardo, Bradley, and Caldwell, 1975; Fogel and Thelen, 1987; Gauvin and Rogoff, 1989; Jennings and Connors, 1989; Power and Parke, 1983; Rogoff, 1990; Spangler, 1989). This research has focused primarily on cognitive development in older children, but its extension to younger ages is of great interest, and its applicability to play research plausible.

The concurrent associations between adult behaviors and child play described above indicate that (1) children are receptive to parental suggestions and positive social interactions within the play setting; (2) children play at higher levels with a more sophisticated partner than when playing alone, a difference attributable directly to children's responses to parental prompts; and (3) certain types of social and didactic interactions and characteristics of the caregiver-child relationship are associated with child play ability—most notably, the social domain of caregiver behaviors relates to child play that is symbolic. These findings provide a reasonable basis for future research using play to assess the role of parents in cognitive development. Yet, these concurrent associations do not imply causal mechanisms, and there is no research that directly supports the idea that parental involvement in play enhances either skills outside of the dyadic setting or later cognitive functioning (Fein, 1981; Sachs, 1984).

Experimental studies have demonstrated increased levels of play sophistication in children after modeling, and they indicate that children are able to take what they have learned from a more sophisticated partner to play outside the dyad, provided that the modeled play does not far outreach the level of play that the child was capable of alone (Bretherton, O'Connell, Shore, and Bates, 1984; Fenson and Ramsey, 1981). However, these studies have only looked at very short-term effects of such modeling. A longitudinal examination of Vibbert and Bornstein's (1989) data did not reveal any long-term effects of parental behaviors on child play. Bornstein, Vibbert, Tal, and O'Donnell (1992) found that neither mothers' nor fathers' social or didactic behaviors alone or in interaction with one another at thirteen months predicted child play at twenty months. In another study, the positive correlations between thirteen-month maternal demonstrations and solicitations of play and twenty-month child play dropped out when level of child play at thirteen and twenty months was controlled (Tamis-LeMonda and Bornstein, 1991). Finally, research reported elsewhere in this volume (see Sigman and Sena) indicates that play development has a strong maturational component: Preterm infants play at less sophisticated levels when matched to term children of the same postnatal age, but they play at similar levels when their age is corrected for differences in length of gestation.

More research on the stability of child play and the predictive validity of early play measures for later cognitive development is also needed. Stability of child play over even short periods of development has not been demonstrated (Tamis-LeMonda and Bornstein, 1991), and only the lack of advancement to symbolic play levels has been shown to put children at risk for later intellectual functioning (McDonald, Sigman, and Ungerer, 1989; Sigman, McDonald, Neumann, and Bwibo, 1991). Future research should focus on specific associations between types of play and subsequent ability (Bornstein, 1989; Vibbert and Bornstein, 1989; Wachs, 1987; Wachs and Chan, 1986), as for example in relations between role play and discourse or narrative skills (Sachs, 1984). In addition, bidirectional (parent-to-child and child-to-parent) and indirect influences have to be considered, factors that have proved very difficult to untangle in other areas of early cognitive development (see Yoder and Kaiser, 1989). It is clear that there is much work yet to be done before we have answers to questions concerning the impact of differential parental behaviors on subsequent child cognitive abilities within the domain of play. However, the potential reward of such an endeavor is manifest based on our current understanding of caregiver-child interaction and play.

References

Baruch, C. "The Influence of the Mother-Child Relationship on the Emergence of Symbolic Play." Poster presented at the biennial meeting of the Society for Research in Child Development, Seattle, April 1991.

Beeghly, M., Perry, B. W., and Cicchetti, D. "Structural and Affective Dimensions of Play Development in Young Children with Down Syndrome." *International Journal of Behavioral Development*, 1989, *12*, 257–277.

Belsky, J., Garduque, L., and Hrncir, E. "Assessing Performance, Competence, and Executive Capacity in Infant Play: Relations to Home Environment and Security of Attachment." *Developmental Psychology*, 1984, 20, 406–417.

Belsky, J., Goode, M. K., and Most, R. K. "Maternal Stimulation and Infant Exploratory Competence: Cross-Sectional, Correlational, and Experimental Analyses." *Child Development*, 1980, 51, 1163–1178.

Belsky, J., and Most, R. K. "From Exploration to Play: A Cross-Sectional Study of Infant Free-Play Behavior." *Developmental Psychology*, 1981, 17, 630–639.

Bornstein, M. H. "Between Caretakers and Their Young: Two Modes of Interaction and Their Consequences for Cognitive Growth." In M. H. Bornstein and J. S. Bruner (eds.), *Interaction in Human Development*. Hillsdale, N.J.: Erlbaum, 1989.

Bornstein, M. H., Vibbert, M., Tal, J., and O'Donnell, K. "Toddler Language and Play in the Second Year: Stability, Covariation, and Influences of Parenting." *First Language*, 1992, 12, 323–338.

Bradley, R. H., and Caldwell, B. M. "174 Children: A Study of the Relationship Between Home Environment and Cognitive Development During the First Five Years." In A. W. Gottfried (ed.), *Home Environment and Early Cognitive Development*. San Diego: Academic Press, 1984.

Bretherton, I., and Bates, E. "The Development of Representation from 10 to 28 Months: Differential Stability of Language and Symbolic Play." In R. W. Emde and R. J. Harmon (eds.), *Continuities and Discontinuities in Development*. New York: Plenum, 1984.

Bretherton, I., O'Connell, B., Shore, C., and Bates, E. "The Effect of Contextual Variation on Symbolic Play: Development from 20 to 28 Months." In I. Bretherton (ed.), *Symbolic Play: The Development of Social Understanding*. San Diego: Academic Press, 1984.

Bruner, J. S. "The Pragmatics of Acquisition." In W. Deutsch (ed.), *The Child's Construction of Language*. San Diego: Academic Press, 1981.

Carew, J. V. *Experience and the Development of Intelligence in Young Children at Home and in Day Care*. Monographs of the Society for Research in Child Development, vol. 45, nos. 6–7 (serial no. 187). Chicago: University of Chicago Press, 1980.

Clarke-Stewart, K. A. *Interactions Between Mothers and Their Young Children: Characteristics and Consequences*. Monographs of the Society for Research in Child Development, vol. 38, nos. 6–7 (serial no. 153). Chicago: University of Chicago Press, 1973.

Dixon, W. E., and Shore, C. "Measuring Symbolic Play Style in Infancy: A Methodological Approach." Paper presented at the biennial meeting of the International Conference on Infant Studies, Montreal, Quebec, Canada, April 1990.

Dunn, J., and Wooding, C. "Play in the Home and Its Implications for Learning." In B. Tizard and D. Harvey (eds.), *The Biology of Play*. Philadelphia: Lippincott, 1977.

Eckerman, C. O., and Didow, S. M. "Toddlers' Social Coordinations: Changing Responses to Another's Invitation to Play." *Developmental Psychology*, 1989, 25, 794–804.

Elardo, R., Bradley, R., and Caldwell, B. M. "The Relation of Infants' Home Environments to Mental Test Performance from Six to Thirty-Six Months: A Longitudinal Analysis." *Child Development*, 1975, 46, 71–76.

Fein, G. G. "Pretend Play in Childhood: An Integrative Review." *Child Development*, 1981, 52, 1095–1118.

Fenson, L., and Ramsey, D. S. "Decentration and Integration of the Child's Play in the Second Year." *Child Development*, 1980, 51, 171–178.

Fiese, B. "Playful Relationships: A Contextual Analysis of Mother-Toddler Interaction and Symbolic Play." *Child Development*, 1990, 61, 1648–1656.

Fogel, A., and Thelen, E. "Development of Early Expressive and Communicative Action: Reinterpreting the Evidence from a Dynamic Systems Perspective." *Developmental Psychology*, 1987, 23, 747–761.

Gauvin, M., and Rogoff, B. "Collaborative Problem Solving and Children's Planning Skills." *Developmental Psychology*, 1989, 25, 139–151.

Göncü, A. "The Role of Adults and Peers in the Socialization of Play During the Preschool Years." In G. Casto, S. Ascione, and M. Salehi (eds.), *Current Perspectives in Infancy and Early Childhood Research.* Logan, Utah: Early Intervention Research Institute Press, 1987.

Goodwyn, S. W., Acredolo, L. P., and Fulmer, A. H. "Mother-Infant Play Behavior as a Predictor of Language Development: A Longitudinal Study from 11 to 24 Months." Poster presented at the biennial meeting of the International Conference on Infant Studies, Miami, Florida, April 1992.

Green, J. A., Gustafson, G. E., and West, M. J. "Effects of Infant Development on Mother-Infant Interaction." *Child Development,* 1980, *51,* 199–207.

Howes, C., and Stewart, P. "Child's Play with Adults, Toys, and Peers: An Examination of Family and Child-Care Influences." *Developmental Psychology,* 1987, *23,* 423–430.

Jennings, K. D., and Connors, R. E. "Mothers' Interactional Style and Children's Competence at Three Years." *International Journal of Behavioral Development,* 1989, *12,* 155–175.

Klein, P. S. "Stability and Change in Interaction of Israeli Mothers and Infants." *Infant Behavior and Development,* 1988, *11,* 55–70.

McCune-Nicolich, L. "Toward Symbolic Functioning: Structure of Early Pretend Games and Potential Parallels with Language." *Child Development,* 1981, *52,* 785–797.

McDonald, M. A., Sigman, M. D., and Ungerer, J. A. "Intelligence and Behavior Problems in Five-Year-Olds in Relation to Representational Abilities in the Second Year of Life." *Journal of Developmental and Behavioral Pediatrics,* 1989, *10,* 86–91.

Matas, L., Arend, R., and Sroufe, L. A. "Continuity of Adaptation in the Second Year: The Relationship Between Quality of Attachment and Later Competence." *Child Development,* 1978, *49,* 547–556.

Miller, C., and Garvey, C. "Mother-Baby Role Play." In I. Bretherton (ed.), *Symbolic Play: The Development of Social Understanding.* San Diego: Academic Press, 1984.

Nicolich, L. M. "Beyond Sensorimotor Intelligence: Assessment of Symbolic Maturity Through Analysis of Pretend Play." *Merrill-Palmer Quarterly,* 1977, *23,* 89–99.

O'Connell, B., and Bretherton, I. "Toddlers' Play, Alone and with Mother: The Role of Maternal Guidance." In I. Bretherton (ed.), *Symbolic Play: The Development of Social Understanding.* San Diego: Academic Press, 1984.

Power, T. G., and Parke, R. "Patterns of Mother and Father Play with Their Eight-Month-Old Infant: A Multiple Analyses Approach." *Infant Behavior and Development,* 1983, *6,* 453–459.

Rogoff, B. *Apprenticeship in Thinking: Cognitive Development in Social Context.* New York: Oxford University Press, 1990.

Rogoff, B., Malkin, C., and Gilbride, K. "Interaction with Babies as Guidance in Development." In B. Rogoff and J. V. Wertsch (eds.), *Children's Learning in the Zone of Proximal Development.* New Directions for Child Development, no. 23. San Francisco: Jossey-Bass, 1984.

Ruff, H. A. "Infants' Manipulative Exploration of Objects: Effects of Age and Object Characteristics." *Developmental Psychology,* 1984, *20,* 9–20.

Sachs, J. "The Role of Adult-Child Play in Language Development." In K. Rubin (ed.), *Children's Play.* New Directions in Child Development, no. 9. San Francisco: Jossey-Bass, 1980.

Sachs, J. "Children's Play and Communicative Development." In R. L. Schiefelbusch and J. Pickar (eds.), *The Acquisition of Communicative Competence.* Baltimore: University Park Press, 1984.

Sigman, M. D. "What Are the Core Deficits in Autism?" In S. H. Broman and J. Graffman (eds.), *Atypical Cognitive Deficits in Developmental Disorders: Implications for Brain Function.* Hillsdale, N.J.: Erlbaum, in press.

Sigman, M. D., McDonald, M. A., Neumann, C., and Bwibo, N. "Prediction of Cognitive Competence in Kenyan Children from Toddler Nutrition, Family Characteristics, and Abilities." *Journal of Child Psychology and Psychiatry and Allied Disciplines,* 1991, *32,* 307–320.

Sigman, M. D., and others. "Home Interactions and the Development of Embu Toddlers in Kenya." *Child Development,* 1988, *59,* 1251–1261.

Slade, A. "A Longitudinal Study of Maternal Involvement and Symbolic Play During the Toddler Period." *Child Development,* 1987a, *58,* 367–375.

Slade, A. "Quality of Attachment and Early Symbolic Play." *Developmental Psychology,* 1987b, *23,* 78–85.

Spangler, G. "Toddlers' Everyday Experiences as Related to Preceding Mental and Emotional Disposition and Their Relationship to Subsequent Mental and Motivational Development: A Short-Term Longitudinal Study." *International Journal of Behavioral Development,* 1989, *12,* 285–303.

Spenser, P. E., and Deyo, D. A. "Cognitive and Social Aspects of Deaf Children's Play." M. Marschark and M. D. Clark (eds.), *Psychological Perspectives on Deafness.* Hillsdale, N.J.: Erlbaum, 1993.

Tamis-LeMonda, C. S., and Bornstein, M. H. "Habituation and Maternal Encouragement of Attention in Infancy as Predictors of Toddler Language, Play, and Representational Competence." *Child Development,* 1989, *60,* 738–751.

Tamis-LeMonda, C. S., and Bornstein, M. H. "Language, Play, and Attention at One Year." *Infant Behavior and Development,* 1990, *13,* 85–98.

Tamis-LeMonda, C. S., and Bornstein, M. H. "Individual Variation, Correspondence, Stability, and Change in Mother and Toddler Play." *Infant Behavior and Development,* 1991, *14,* 143–162.

Tamis-LeMonda, C. S., and others. "Language and Play at One Year: A Comparison of Toddlers and Mothers in the United States and Japan." *International Journal of Behavioral Development,* 1992, *15,* 19–42.

Tingley, E. C., and Golden, R. M. "Sequence and Structure of Symbolic Play Between Well and Depressed Mothers and Their Toddlers." Poster presented at the biennial meeting of the International Conference on Infant Studies, Miami, Florida, April 1992.

Unger, O., and Howes, C. "Mother-Child Interactions and Symbolic Play Between Toddlers and Their Adolescent or Mentally Retarded Mothers." *Occupational Therapy Journal of Research,* 1988, *8,* 237–249.

Ungerer, J. A., and Sigman, M. D. "The Relation of Play and Sensorimotor Behavior to Language in the Second Year." *Child Development,* 1984, *55,* 1440–1455.

Ungerer, J. A., Zelazo, P. R., Kearsley, R. B., and O'Leary, K. "Developmental Changes in the Representation of Objects in Symbolic Play from 18 to 34 Months of Age." *Child Development,* 1981, *52,* 186–195.

Vibbert, M., and Bornstein, M. H. "Specific Associations Between Domains of Mother-Child Interaction and Toddler Referential Language and Pretense Play." *Infant Behavior and Development,* 1989, *12,* 163–184.

Vygotsky, L. S. *Mind in Society: The Development of Higher Psychological Processes.* (M. Cole, V. John-Steiner, S. Scribner, and E. Souberman, eds. and trans.). Cambridge, Mass.: Harvard University Press, 1978.

Wachs, T. D. "Proximal Experience and Early Cognitive Intellectual Development: The Social Environment." In A. Gottfried (ed.), *Home Environment and Mental Development.* San Diego: Academic Press, 1984.

Wachs, T. D. "Specificity of Environmental Action as Manifest in Environmental Correlates of Infants' Mastery Motivation." *Developmental Psychology,* 1987, *23,* 782–790.

Wachs, T. D., and Chan, A. "Specificity of Environmental Action, as Seen in Environmental Correlates of Infants' Communication Performance." *Child Development,* 1986, *57,* 1464–1474.

Werner, H., and Kaplan, B. *Symbol Formation.* New York: Wiley, 1963.

Wertsch, J. V. "From Social Interaction to Higher Psychological Processes: A Clarification and Application of Vygotsky's Theory." *Human Development,* 1979, *22,* 1–22.

Yoder, P. J., and Kaiser, A. P. "Alternative Explanations for the Relationship Between Maternal Verbal Interaction Style and Child Language Development." *Journal of Child Language*, 1989, *16*, 141–160.

Zukow, P. G. "The Relationship Between Interaction with the Caregiver and the Emergence of Play Activities During the One-Word Period." *British Journal of Developmental Psychology*, 1986, *4*, 223–234.

ANNE WATSON O'REILLY *is postdoctoral fellow in Child and Family Research at the National Institute of Child Health and Human Development, Bethesda, Maryland. Her interests include early cognitive development and language acquisition.*

MARC H. BORNSTEIN *is senior research scientist and head of Child and Family Research at the National Institute of Child Health and Human Development. His interests include experimental, methodological, comparative, developmental, cross-cultural, and aesthetic psychology.*

Children develop the capacity for consciousness of self and other as mental representation becomes an alternative intentional state distinct from perception.

The Development of Play as the Development of Consciousness

Loraine McCune

How might an organism initially attuned to the perceptual world (Gibson, 1969; Ruff, 1978) come to acquire differential perceptual and representational capacities? One might even wonder, as has Leslie (1987), how counterfactual representational processes such as pretending can be prevented from threatening children's developing knowledge of reality. Children's early acquisition of knowledge arises through play that is at first limited to sensory and motor activities. Around one year of age, the child's repertoire begins to expand to include representational play. Premack and Woodruff (1978) linked the notions of deceit and pretense in an effort to identify which abilities distinguish an organism that is conscious of its own mind, as separate from other minds, from an organism that is not. They characterized such knowledge of self and other as a "theory of mind." Leslie (1987) suggested that this knowledge arises suddenly due to the new ability to "decouple" various mental contents. This contrasts with the position that consciousness of the mental states of self and other arises gradually with the development of mental representation (Werner and Kaplan, 1963).

The thesis of this chapter is that the capacity for consciousness of self and other is an outgrowth of the capacity for representational as well as perceptual activities, especially activities of both types that can be characterized as "play." Consciousness entails awareness of self as experiencer

I thank Edith Neimark for the influential insights gained through collaboration with her on a joint presentation to the Society for Philosophy and Psychology regarding representational play and theory of mind.

67

and the capacity to direct attention to either perceptual information or representational experience. Both aspects of consciousness, by definition, involve directed intentional states (Dennet, 1991; Piaget, [1932] 1973; Sartre, [1948] 1966) under voluntary control of the subject.

Consciousness of Self and Other

Human infants depend on a consistently caring partner for their health and well-being. (They die or fail to develop adequately without such care.) Thus, all human infants who make the transition to representational consciousness do so in relation to a partner. The most radical proposal for the role of the infant's partner is presented by Werner and Kaplan (1963), who claimed that the infant's motivation for this development is the need to prevent the sense of separateness that arises as the infant begins to experience self and other as distinct.

Indeed, children's understanding of absent realities, which requires representational processing, shows a well-documented developmental course that is specifically observable in play and that culminates in new skills at eighteen to twenty-four months of age (McCune-Nicolich, 1981; Nicolich, 1977; Užgiris and Hunt, 1969). During a similar age range, there is considerable growth in the sense of a self and increasing awareness of the distinction between self and other (Amsterdam, 1972; Lewis and Brooks, 1975; Mahler, Bergman, and Pine, 1975; Stern, 1985). It would seem that affective and cognitive aspects of development are intertwined in this period of growth.

According to Schachtel (1954, p. 318), both affective needs and "a distinctly human capacity for object interest" provide the means for the development of consciousness of self and other in an objective world. "Focal attention is the tool, the distinctly human equipment, by means of which the capacity for object interest can be realized" (p. 318). Schachtel credited the experience of repeated acts of focal attention with bringing about the infant's consciousness of self in a world of objects and considered acts of focal attention in play with mother as the most powerful vehicle for developing consciousness. Similarly, Werner and Kaplan (1963) described emergent consciousness as tripartite—involving self, objects, and mother.

The capacity for focal attention involves a voluntary directedness to stimulus information, that is, a perceptual intention. This contrasts with earlier perceptual experience, which is responsive and reactive to stimulus properties. The first object of focal attention is the mother's face, which is explored visually from birth and manually beginning with the child's ability for directed reaching. An infant's waking hours are spent with a caregiver who observes and interprets the child's experience. These observations yield an intuitive sense of the infant's readiness to explore and the focus of his or her interest. This common history and resulting subtle aspects of mutual understanding promote the possibility of shared attentional focus when the child begins exploration of objects.

The course of perceptual exploration of objects tends from the beginning to favor the development of representation. As a child examines an object, multiple acts of focal attention (where the object is sequentially rotated, fingered, shaken) present the child with varied perceptual experiences that nevertheless relate to the same object (Ruff, 1986). The process of engaged focal attention exposes the child to aspects of an object that vary and that entail "absence to view" of one side of the object as the child rotates it to consider the other side. The constant in these situations is the self as experiencer.

Thus, as the children's central nervous systems undergo development that might allow more advanced cognitive processes, their interest in the world exposes them to situations that include opportunities for experiencing the alternating presence and absence of particular perceptual experiences of objects. When children drop things accidentally, and later with intent, they directly experience the temporary disappearance of objects. When children engage in peek-a-boo, they express their interest in the notions of absence and presence as applied to persons. By virtue of these experiences, the developing child extends perception to the recent past and to the near future, gradually developing the distinction between perceptual experiences that rely on sensorimotor focal attention and representational experiences that extend beyond the sensorimotor, requiring focal attention to internal processes. In representational play, children exhibit growing control over this distinction.

As the child experiences the self as separate from mother and objects, Werner and Kaplan (1963, p. 42) claim that within an essential "primordial sharing situation" objects become a vehicle for maintaining a sense of unity in the dyad. This process takes place at first through joint contemplation of objects, involving perceptual approaches to the world, and later through participation in representational play and language. The "distance" of the representational contents from the perceptual context may be an index of the capacity for awareness of psychological separation between self and other. Changes in treatment of the mother in the play situation as representational play develops provide evidence for this thesis. Thus, the capacity for representation is posed as correlative with the affective capacity for psychological separation.

Perceptual Versus Representational Intentions

According to Sartre ([1948] 1966), consciousness is characterized by a certain "intention" and a certain knowledge that is inseparable from the intention. In perceptual consciousness, the intention is to experience observable reality. For example, a perceptual approach to a photograph may serve aesthetic or informational purposes. In contrast, the representational intention might be to envision a friend, as she is known, with the photograph as a starting point. If the photograph is then examined to determine the color of the friend's eyes, a perceptual intention characterizes this activity. The "object" of perception is the photograph, but the object of representation is, as Sartre notes, "nothingness." The representational consciousness is "a consciousness of my friend Jane," but it is an internal process, directed at no physical or mental entity.

As adults, we recognize that perceptual, exploratory processes serve the acquisition of knowledge, whereas representation permits contemplation of what is known (Sartre, [1948] 1966). If, for example, one is unsure of the location of San Francisco, the solution is not to invoke an image of the state of California. Rather one consults a map. In order to reexperience former pleasures enjoyed there, on the other hand, one need only turn the mind to the contemplation of those pleasures.

Schachtel (1954) associated the eventual capacity to keep hold of an idea in thought, that is, to develop focal attention to the *idea of an object in its absence,* to a developing understanding of the retrievability of objects (including the mother) and their continued existence and eventual return, even in cases when they are not available for exploration or need satisfaction. According to Schachtel, the maintenance of a representational consciousness is effortful: "A formal act of will is needed to maintain the image as opposed to perception. Gliding from one to the other occurs from time to time" (1954, p. 37). Thus, knowledge is not threatened by imagination. Rather the perceptual world provides continuous potential distraction from internal representational states.

Sensorimotor Exploration Versus Play

Piaget (1962) distinguished activities such as examination of objects to gain knowledge about the world from play, which expresses what is already known. When the sensorimotor infant examines objects, the intentional focus is perceptual and the knowledge is supplied by this contact with physical reality. In contrast, Piaget (1962, p. 162) characterizes sensorimotor play as follows: "In a word, he repeats his behavior, not in any further effort to learn or investigate, but for the mere joy of mastering it and showing off to himself his own power of subduing reality." Repetition is a form of "re-presentation" at a sensory and motor level for the purposes of reexperiencing the known.

Sensorimotor play is limited to the perceptual plane and may culminate in additional exploration of objects. In contrast, representational play is the expression of knowledge gained through experience or observation. It therefore involves the reenactment of a previous event with the potential for either partner to embellish the portrayal. Such extensions broaden the representational experience and enhance the potential for the partners to experience similar intentional states.

It is in the course of playful construction and vocal exchange that the mother or other trusted adult can offer knowledge from the foundation of her own representational intention to attract the infant into an increasing capacity for representational consciousness. As the baby portrays a pretend event in action, or displays an object of interest, the mother comments, providing linguistic and conceptual knowledge. The overt acts of play and the availability of correlative language (Vygotsky, [1934] 1962) become the means of maintaining representational focus. Mahler, Bergman, and Pine (1975) observed that mothers' brief absences from their one-year-old children led to reduction of the children's interest in play, and apparently inwardly concentrated attention, as each child held a favorite toy or remained near the chair where his or her mother had been sitting. The effort of maintaining representational consciousness is eased by the mother's presence and implicit sharing of the infant's focus of attention.

Representational Play

Representational play develops during the second year of life, offering a reliable indicator of the child's developing representational consciousness. It thus provides a useful vehicle for examining knowledge of self and other as well as the gradual differentiation of representational consciousness from dependence on perceptual reality (decontextualization). On the one hand, the experience of shared consciousness with a valued caregiver, usually the mother, is considered a motivator for representation. On the other hand, the mother is credited with the role of partner in the child's gradual transition to a broad capacity for representational thought. Examination of the interpsychic and intrapsychic aspects of representational play with mother illustrates this thesis.

The term *representational play* is used with reference to the full range of play acts that represent realistic activities. We think of a symbol as standing in for a meaning separate and different from itself. For play to be defined as symbolic in this sense, the acts of play should function for the child in support of a representational consciousness of the events conveyed by the motor acts of play. Alternatively, representations may convey information to an observer, without reference to the child's internal experience (Van Gulick, 1982). In the course of development, motor acts at first represent events in an information-exhibiting sense. Later, these same acts are executed in a manner indicating that the child's enactments are symbolic, referring to mental contents necessarily different from the acts themselves. In the developmental course of representational play, subtle but universal changes in the manner in which play acts are produced give evidence of an orderly change in accompanying internal states. The universality of this developmental sequence of changes in behaviors that are superficially similar is sufficient rationale for maintaining a single term for the sequence as a whole. Distinctions within the sequence should be made on strong theoretical and empirical grounds (Huttenlocher and Higgins, 1978; McCune-Nicolich, 1981).

Clearly, inferences concerning likely mental states underlying observed play behavior are essential to determining the representational status of that play. By addressing the course of play from the perspective of underlying states, I show here that advanced symbolic play or pretending is a consequence of precursors. With successive developments such play depends less and less on the perceptual context for support (decontextualization). Concomitantly, the child shows increasing evidence of intuitive understanding of mental states in the self and the play partner. Table 6.1 summarizes five levels of representational play previously established (McCune, 1992b; McCune-Nicolich, 1981) and indicates concomitant changes in presumed mental state, decontextualization, and intuitive recognition of the mental state of the play partner.

Recognitory Gestures with Objects. Between nine and fifteen months of age, children first appropriately use conventional objects out of context (Level 1). These acts are termed *presymbolic schemes* to indicate both their relation with later symbolic acts and their limitation to sensorimotor expression of meaning. As the child touches cup to lips, or comb to hair, briefly and with serious demeanor, there is little reason to suspect that the infant is aware of the representational relation between the action and past real experiences. It is more parsimonious to assume that the child is exercising an established scheme related to a familiar object. Such play is representational in that it can be seen by an observer to express in mime the activity of drinking. Engagement in such acts, which derive from imitation of self or other, provides the bridge from perceptual motor action to mental representation (Piaget and Inhelder, 1969). Furthermore, such acts provide child and adult with a present perceptual and motor context that has the potential for shared reference to absent reality. Such acts take place in the absence of their usual function, but they are abbreviated renditions of such realistic activities and hence are not differentiated from the acts that they represent (McCune, 1987). At this same level, children recognize the functions of toy objects, such as telephones and trucks, without indicating representational consciousness of the relation of their play to the actual function of the objects that these replicas represent.

Self-Pretend. Between twelve and eighteen months, the child begins to make reference to the similar past experiences underlying play acts by elaborating the simple actions of play in a manner that makes them more like the (presumably) internally represented experience that now guides them (Level 2). The child makes eating sounds and exaggerated gestures,

Table 6.1. Stages of Differentiation of Representation from Sensorimotor Stimulus Support as Shown at Play

Play Level	Presumed Mental State	Decontextualization	Self-Other Understanding
1. Child places cup or other round concave object in appropriate orientation to lip	Sensorimotor awareness of tactile and visual aspect of the object and movement of the body	Sensorimotor action removed in time from corresponding real activity	No evidence
2. Child makes drinking sounds with cup to lips; throws back head, swallows; smiles to mother and repeats these actions as she watches	Consciousness of habitual meaningful act and its details supported by the tactile and visual aspects of the objects and movements of the body	Removal in time and evidence of awareness of the relationship of the representational and real activities as child compensates for absent aspects by simulating them	Attempts to ensure shared awareness of meanings
3. Child "feeds" mother or doll; child offers phone to mother then watches her use it	Awareness of meaningful acts as general to animates; contemplation of variations in agent and action; events supported by tactile or visual aspects	Loss of dependence on bodily action by the self	Direct evidence that the other can participate in the same experience as the self
4. Child stirs absent liquid in cup with spoon; feeds mother; feeds doll, feeds mother; feeds doll again; stirs again, offers doll and spoon to mother; watches mother feed doll	Contemplation of multiple aspects of an event; more complete understanding of of an event supported by multiple actions	Representation less dependent on sensorimotor action as the child can shift among actions as the symbolic vehicle for maintaining internal representation; one representational meaning can suggest another	Alternation of activities with others suggests increased interest in coordinating joint perspective; child uses maternal suggestions
5. Child takes doll, searches for bottle, then feeds doll; child says "tea" then drinks from empty cup; child places banana to ear as telephone	Consciousness of representational possibility precedes the motor act; additional symbolic meanings may arise in the course of play	Source of the activity is mental rather than motor or visual; significance of objects can shift as new meanings occur to the child; accepts decontextualized suggestions from mother; can pretend in absence of any symbolic surrogate	Simultaneous awareness of representational and real meanings; intentionally, "1 am using this banana as a telephone."

such as tossing the head back to drink, that mimic the consumatory behaviors of real drinking and thus refer to the absent past. These kinds of actions indicate the child's beginning awareness of the partial resemblance and representational differentiation that link the play act and the realistic event that it represents (McCune, 1987). Typically, the child solicits maternal attention to these acts more than to other forms of pay (Dunn and Wooding, 1977; Slade, 1987), showing a consciousness that the adult mind also can join the focus on absent events. Some analyses do not consider such "evidence of pretending" in evaluating play acts and would probably include self-directed presymbolic acts in this category.

Decentered Pretend. Piaget (1962) noted that pretending is at first limited to events experienced by the child and expressed with a focus on the self. By fifteen to twenty months, children begin to extend their play beyond these situations. They give drinks to dolls, say "hi" when playing with toy telephones, and make engine noises as they move vehicle replicas in careful patterns. All of these examples show characteristics of Level 3, both reference to the "real" event as experienced in the past and extension of the representational consciousness beyond the child's own body or activities (McCune, 1987). When evidence of pretending is not considered as a criterion for judging the maturity of play, categories of object-directed and other-directed pretend include both Level 1 and Level 3 acts as described here.

An infant's request that mother engage in a representational play act constitutes direct evidence of the expectation that mother's representational consciousness can be influenced. However, there is clear dependence on external play activities as the vehicle for mother and baby to generate and maintain this joint representational state.

Linear Representational Play Combinations. Play soon develops a sequential character (Level 4, fifteen to twenty-four months), with the baby stringing play acts together or mothers and infants taking turns in such acts as drinking from a cup and pretending to talk on the telephone. In such sequences, one act may suggest the next. However, the ability to shift from one act to another in representing a complex event indicates a further differentiation of the representational consciousness from its perceptual-motor support (McCune, 1987). The infants, by playing in representational sequences with mothers, present themselves with external perceptually bound material that makes reference to absent reality. Parents and older siblings become ready collaborators in this endeavor. Thus, in the context of representational play there is a shared evocation of absent realities.

Hierarchical Representational Play Combinations. Reliance on the perceptual world is significantly reduced when the child indicates that a prior internal act guides the representational play act (Level 5). For Piaget (1962), such a prior act defines the play as symbolic. Whereas earlier play acts seem to arise directly from the situation perceived by the child, now a hierarchical structure is apparent where an internal prior act provides meaning for the pretend activity. Because a purely mental act separate from perceptual reality is now represented by the child, the motor performance can be considered symbolic in the sense of standing in for a meaning other than itself.

Three forms of hierarchically organized play have been identified based on the inference that they are directed by a prior mental act: (1) object substitution, (2) treating a doll (or other replica) as "active," and (3) other representational acts where the child's behavior indicates that a prior "plan" is the source of the activity. Just as the modifications of the child's behavior between Levels 1 and 2 reveal initial evocation of the absent, close attention to the context of play acts at Level 5 indicates that their source is representational rather than perceptual. Even at this level, however, the child does not abandon environmental support, preferring realistic props. It is necessary to look for evidence of a "prior mental act" or plan that guides the behavior. Supporting evidence includes preparatory activities, search for appropriate objects, announced object substitution, or verbal statement of a plan. The action of having a doll enact a behavior (for example, moving its arm so that it drinks, rather than holding the cup to its lips) indicates a prior mental act defining the doll as "animate." At this level, the term *symbolic play* is generally accepted (Huttenlocher and Higgins, 1978; Piaget, 1962).

Mechanisms for the Transition to Mental Representation

During the first years of life, ontological processes, including continued myelination of the nervous system, provide ongoing support for the infant's activities, which in turn influence developmental adequacy, with any developmental outcome best considered as both the product of a dynamic system and a continuing contributor to the system (McCune, 1992a; Thelen, 1989). As noted earlier, situations where mother and baby involve themselves together with objects are considered by Werner and Kaplan (1963) to be the primordial sharing situation. Detailed consideration of the mental states exhibited by children in representational play confirms Schachtel's (1954) view that the action of constructing representational events with mother provides a context for the child's transition to a differentiated representation of self and other in relation to a concrete world.

In considering the transition to symbolic play, Leslie (1987, p. 422) wonders "how perceptual evidence could ever force . . . a young child to infer unobserved mental states," and he considers children's understanding of pretense in others equally mysterious. These developments depend on the capacity for mental representation. This capacity is not fully realized in play until true symbolic play begins (Level 5). Throughout the sequence described in Table 6.1, children's understanding of others' play keeps pace with their own representational abilities. Although parents participate in infant representational play prior to Level 5, the young child's dependence on perceptual reality limits understanding of more advanced adult pretend. The child who is not capable of symbolic substitution (limited to Level 3) is unwilling (or unable) to identify verbally the contents of the empty cup, despite available vocabulary and considerable prompting from a parent ("What are you drinking?" "Is that tea?"). Once children show true symbolic play, they are easily influenced by mature players (Beizer and Howes, 1992). Earlier play with parents provides important opportunities for the development of not only mental representation but also an understanding of the mental states in others.

The shared context and representational action provide the material for shared intentional focus. Mothers and other mature players become models and guides, always limited in their influence by the range of the child's zone of proximal development (Vygotsky, 1978). Internal states are expressed directly in play: "Is the baby hungry?" "Is your baby crying, did she fall down?" At every level, representational play provides a bootstrapping opportunity for the development of representation. Such play with peers provides the opportunity for continued "study" of other minds, as preschool children jointly reinstate common experiences, such as meals, car rides, and bedtime.

Conclusion

As Johnson (1988) aptly notes, the notion that young children's behavioral demonstrations of awareness of the internal states of others constitute a "theory" is an analogy that disregards the abstract nature of theory as applied to scientific thinking. Children's understanding of their own and others' intentional states is an intuitively functioning process that develops gradually with the capacity for mental representation. The development of mental representation entails a phenomenological distinction between perceptual and representational reality that prevents confusion between the two. The capacity for representation helps the child engage with others in a manner that extends beyond perceptual reality.

The "theory of mind" view eliminates this distinction between perception and representation that is so readily experienced in everyday life. According to Perner (1988, p. 169), present awareness of a given situation constitutes a "knowledge base" that can "endure over time, thereby encoding and preserving information about past events." This suggests that processes normally considered perceptual fulfill a representational function. Recognition memory, which is demonstrated from early infancy across the human life span, suggests long-term effects of perceptual experiences. However, such a physiological record constitutes "representation" in the sense of information encoding, as does the genetic information "represented" in a DNA sequence, whereas the ordinary sense of mental representation entails "representation use," that is, functional access to the information represented (Van Gulick, 1982). Leslie (1987) similarly blurs the distinction between perception and representation, using the term *first-order representations* to describe what would ordinarily be termed *perceptual experience* (Johnson, 1988).

In this chapter, I have described ways in which the sophistication of representational play exposes both the child's development toward mental representation and the correlative ability to recognize that representational interaction with mother involves engaging another consciousness (sometimes termed *theory of mind*). It seems clear that there is a continuity over time in these processes, such that the ability to cancel perceptual reality in favor of representation (for example, by pretending that a banana is a telephone) is an outgrowth of earlier processes, rather than a discontinuous development. Indeed, it is this culminating ability, along with the ability to pretend with no object at all, that identifies the child's capacity for mental representation. The child can now experience a perceptual consciousness, intending to gain knowledge from the physical world, or a representational consciousness, intending to contemplate absent realities. Representational consciousness does not remain limited to playful contexts, but with the development of logical operations it functions in the service of reality-directed problem solving as well as fantasy. Children develop the capacity for consciousness of self and other as mental representation becomes an alternative intentional state distinct from perception.

References

Amsterdam, B. "Mirror Self-Image Reactions Before Age Two." *Developmental Psychology,* 1972, 5, 297–305.

Beizer, L., and Howes, C. "Mothers and Toddlers: Partners in Early Symbolic Play." In C. Howes, O. Unger, and C. Matheson (eds.), *The Collaborative Construction of Pretend.* Albany: State University of New York Press, 1992.

Dennett, D. *Consciousness Explained.* Boston: Little Brown, 1991.

Dunn, J., and Wooding, C. "Play in the Home and Its Implications for Learning." In B. Tizard and D. Harvey (eds.), *The Biology of Play.* Philadelphia: Lippincott, 1977.

Gibson, E. J. *Principles of Perceptual Learning and Development.* East Norwalk, Conn.: Appleton & Lange, 1969.

Huttenlocher, J., and Higgins, E. T. "Issues in the Study of Symbolic Development." In W. A. Collins (ed.), *Minnesota Symposia on Child Psychology,* vol. 2. Hillsdale, N.J.: Erlbaum, 1978.

Johnson, C. N. "Theory of Mind and the Structure of Conscious Experience." In J. Astington, P. Harris, and D. Olson (eds.), *Developing Theories of Mind.* Cambridge, England: Cambridge University Press, 1988.

Leslie, A. M. "Pretense and Representation: The Origins of 'Theory of Mind.'" *Psychological Review,* 1987, 94, 412–426.

Lewis, M., and Brooks, J. "Infants' Social Perception: A Constructionist View." In L. B. Cohen and P. Salapatek (eds.), *Infant Perception: From Sensation to Cognition*. Vol. 1. San Diego: Academic Press, 1975.

McCune, L. "The Complementary Roles of Differentiation and Integration in the Transition to Symbolization." In J. Montangero, J. Tryphon, and S. Dionnet (eds.), *Symbolism and Knowledge*. Geneva, Switzerland: Fondation Archives Jean Piaget, 1987.

McCune, L. "First Words: A Dynamic Systems View." In C. Ferguson, L. Menn, and C. Stoel-Gammon (eds.), *Phonological Development: Models, Research, Implications*. Parkton, Md.: York Press, 1992a.

McCune, L. "A Normative Study of Representational Play at the Transition to Language." Unpublished manuscript, Rutgers University, 1992b.

McCune-Nicolich, L. "Toward Symbolic Functioning: Structure of Early Pretend Games and Potential Parallels with Language." *Child Development*, 1981, *52*, 785–797.

Mahler, M., Bergman, E., and Pine, F. *The Psychological Birth of the Human Infant*. New York: Basic Books, 1975.

Nicolich, L. M. "Beyond Sensorimotor Intelligence: Assessment of Symbolic Maturity Through Analysis of Pretend Play." *Merrill-Palmer Quarterly*, 1977, *23*, 89–99.

Perner, J. "Developing Semantics for Theories of Mind: From Propositional Attitudes to Mental Representation." In J. Astington, P. Harris, and D. Olson (eds.), *Developing Theories of Mind*. Cambridge, England: Cambridge University Press, 1988.

Piaget, J. *Play, Dreams, and Imitation*. New York: Norton, 1962.

Piaget, J. *The Language and Thought of the Child*. New York: Routledge & Kegan Paul, 1973. (Originally published 1932.)

Piaget, J., and Inhelder, B. *The Psychology of the Child*. New York: Basic Books, 1969.

Premack, D., and Woodruff, G. "Does the Chimpanzee Have a Theory of Mind?" *Behavioral and Brain Sciences*, 1978, *4*, 515–526.

Ruff, H. A. "Infant Recognition of the Invariant Forms of Objects." *Child Development*, 1978, *49*, 293–306.

Ruff, H. A. "Components of Attention During Infants' Manipulative Exploration." *Child Development*, 1986, *57*, 105–114.

Sartre, J.-P. *The Psychology of Imagination*. New York: Philosophical Library, 1966. (Originally published 1948.)

Schachtel, E. G. "The Development of Focal Attention and the Emergence of Reality." *Psychiatry*, 1954, *17*, 309–324.

Slade, A. "A Longitudinal Study of Maternal Involvement and Symbolic Play During the Toddler Period." *Child Development*, 1987, *58*, 367–375.

Stern, D. *The Interpersonal World of the Infant: A View from Psychoanalysis and Developmental Psychology*. New York: Basic Books, 1985.

Thelen, E. "Self-Organization in Developmental Processes: Can Systems Approaches Work?" In M. R. Gunnar and E. Thelen (eds.), *Systems and Development*. Minnesota Symposia on Child Psychology, vol. 22. Hillsdale, N.J.: Erlbaum, 1989.

Uzgiris, I. C., and Hunt, J. *Assessment in Infancy: Ordinal Scales of Psychological Development*. Urbana: University of Illinois Press, 1975.

Van Gulick, R. "Mental Representation: A Functionalist View." *Pacific Philosophical Quarterly*, 1982, *63*, 3–20.

Vygotsky, L. S. *Thought and Language*. (E. Hanfmann and G. Vakar, eds. and trans.) Cambridge, Mass.: MIT Press, 1962. (Originally published 1934.)

Vygotsky, L. S. *Mind in Society: The Development of Higher Psychological Processes*. (M. Cole, V. John-Steiner, S. Scribner, and E. Souberman, eds.) Cambridge, Mass.: Harvard University Press, 1978.

Werner, H., and Kaplan, B. *Symbol Formation*. New York: Wiley, 1963.

Loraine McCune is on the faculty in educational psychology at Rutgers University, New Brunswick, New Jersey. She directs a program in Infant Specialist Interdisciplinary Studies that trains researchers and professionals interested in working with infants and young children (including those with disabilities) and their families.

INDEX

Acredolo, L. P., 57
Activity: of infants, 23–24; nonexploratory, 6–7. *See also* Exploratory activity
Adamson, L. B., 12
Amsterdam, B., 68
Anderson, D. R., 8
Arend, R., 61
Athey, I., 44
Attention: individual differences in, 13–14; measures of, 9–10; and sophistication, 25–26. *See also* Duration of attention; Focused attention
Autistic children, play of, 35–37, 39

Bakeman, R., 12
Balleyguier, C., 49
Baron-Cohen, S., 31, 34, 35, 36
Barrett, D., 47
Baruch, C., 61
Bates, E., 17, 21, 30, 56, 62
Beeghly, M., 34, 60
Beizer, L., 76
Belsky, J., 17, 18, 30, 44, 45, 56, 60, 61
Benroya, S., 35
Bergman, E., 68, 71
Biringin, Z., 32
Bishry, Z., 43
Bond, L., 44
Bornstein, M. H., 1, 3, 10, 11, 13, 17, 18, 19, 20, 22, 23, 28, 30, 37, 50, 55, 56, 57, 58, 59, 60, 62, 66
Boucher, J., 36, 37
Bradley, R., 44, 55, 61
Bretherton, I., 17, 21, 30, 56, 57, 58, 59, 62
Bridges, L., 45
Brierly, L. M., 35
Brooks, J., 68
Brooks-Gunn, J., 34
Bruner, J., 43, 59
Bwibo, N., 29, 33, 60, 62

Caldwell, B. M., 55–56, 61
Campbell, H., 11
Capozzoli, M., 6, 7, 13
Caregivers, 2; child play with, 57–59; and cognitive growth, 61–62; and development, 56–57; fit of style of, 49–50; individual differences in, 59–61; interaction of, with child, 55–56; and variability in play, 44–45. *See also* Mothers
Carew, J. V., 55
Chan, A., 62
Chapieski, M. L., 26, 32, 44
Chavez, A., 47
Children: autistic, 35–37, 39; with disabilities, 37–38; Down syndrome, 34; mentally retarded, 34–35; play of, and caregivers, 55–62. *See also* Infants
Choi, H. P., 8
Cicchetti, D., 34, 60
Clarke-Stewart, K. A., 61
Cognitive assessment, and pretend play, 2, 29–30, 38–39. *See also* Play observations
Cognitive growth, and caregiver, 61–62
Cohen, N., 44
Cohen, S. E., 10
Collard, R., 44
Colombo, J., 10, 11
Combs, T., 49
Competence. *See* Exploratory competence; Representational competence
Connors, R. E., 45, 60, 61
Consciousness: perceptual versus representational, 69–70, 77; play as development of, 3; of self and other, 68–69
Correlates of play, 2; biological, 47–49; environmental, 44–47; individual differences, 49–50; for pre-term infants, 32–33
Cyphers, L., 17

Davenport, R., 44
Dennett, D., 68
Denson, S., 32
Derryberry, D., 13
Development: and changes in play, 56–57; and indexes of play, 21–22; and progression of play, 30–31
Deyo, D. A., 60
Didow, S. M., 57
Dine, K., 17
Dixon, W. E., 18, 57
Down syndrome children, play of, 34

Dubiner, K., 6, 7, 13
Dunn, J., 55, 56, 58, 59, 74
Duration of attention, 18–19, 25–26; change in, and development, 22; and context, 10–13; infant antecedents of, 23–24; and language, 20–21; and level of sophistication, 22; and mental abilities, 22–23. *See also* Attention; Focused attention

Eckerman, C. O., 57
Egypt, study of play in, 45–49
Elardo, R., 61
Ellis, M., 44
Escalona, S., 49
Examining, 6
Exploration, 46; sensorimotor, 70–71
Exploratory activity, 5–6; and focused attention, 7–9; learning during, 6–7; and measures of attention, 9–10
Exploratory competence, 24, 38; with autism, 35; with Down syndrome, 34; and infant activity and habituation, 24; with mental retardation, 34–35; of pre-term infants, 32
Exploratory play, 1. *See also* Exploratory activity; Manipulative play

Fagot, B., 50
Farver, J. M., 31
Fein, G., 17, 44, 49, 50, 61
Fenson, L., 21, 56, 62
Fiese, B., 59
Finck, D., 49
Fitzmaurice, G., 17
Fletcher, J., 32
Focused attention, 7, 14; and context, 10–13; resistance to distraction during, 8–9. *See also* Attention; Duration of attention
Fogel, A., 61
Frodi, A., 45
Fulmer, A. H., 57
Functional play, 46

Galal, O., 43
Gandour, M., 49
Gardner, H., 49, 50
Garduque, L., 61
Garvey, C., 43, 56
Gauvin, M., 61

Gibbs, E., 44
Gibson, E. J., 67
Gilbride, K., 56
Goldberg, S., 11
Golden, R. M., 60
Göncü, A., 56
Goode, M. K., 17, 44, 60
Goodwyn, S. W., 57
Gould, L., 35
Grantham-McGregor, S., 47
Green, J. A., 55
Greenfield, D., 47
Grolnick, W., 45
Gustafson, G. E., 55

Hampson, J., 17
Harmon, R. J., 32
Harris, P. L., 39
Harrison, G., 43
Henderson, B., 44
Hermelin, B., 35
Higgins, E. T., 72, 75
Hill, P. M., 34
Howes, C., 31, 45, 59, 60, 76
Hrncir, E., 61
Hunt, J., 68
Huttenlocher, J., 72, 75

Indexes of play, 2, 17–19, 24–26; association of, 22; change in, and development, 21–22; infant antecedents of, 23–24; and language, 19–21; and mental abilities, 22–23
Individual differences: in attention, 13–14; in caregivers, 59–61; correlates for, 49–50; in play of high-risk infants, 31–33
Infants: activity of, 23–24; attention of, and sophistication, 25–26; habituation of, 24; mildly malnourished, 33; preterm, 31–33. *See also* Children
Inhelder, B., 72

Japan, symbolic play in, 60
Jennings, K. D., 7, 14, 30, 45, 60, 61
Jerome, N., 43
Johnson, C. N., 76, 77
Johnson, M. H., 13

Kahana-Kalman, R., 17
Kahneman, D., 9

Kaiser, A. P., 62
Kaplan, B., 56, 67, 68, 69, 75
Kasari, C., 34, 35
Kearsley, R. B., 56
Kenya, study of play in, 33, 47–49
Kirksey, N., 43
Klein, L. S., 35
Klein, P. S., 56
Kopp, C. B., 30, 32, 34
Krakow, J. B., 30, 32, 34

Landry, S. H., 32, 44
Langmeier, J., 49
Language: of children with disabilities, 37–38; and play, 19–21
Lawson, K. R., 6
Learning, during exploratory activity, 6–7
Lécuyer, R., 11
Leibel, R., 47
Leslie, A. M., 31, 39, 67, 75, 78
Level of sophistication, 18–19, 24–25; antecedents of, 23–24; change in, and development, 21–22; and duration of attention, 22; and language, 20–21; and mental abilities, 22–23
Lewis, M., 11, 34, 47, 68
Lewis, V., 36, 37
Lorch, E. P., 8

MacArthur Communicative Development Inventories, 21
McCabe, G., 43
McCall, R., 43
McCune, L., 3, 21, 67, 72, 74, 75, 79
McCune-Nicolich, L., 17, 18, 34, 56, 68, 72
McDonald, M. A., 33, 60, 62
McGrath, M. P., 26
McNew, S., 17
McQuiston, S., 45
MacTurk, R. H., 32
Mahler, M., 68, 71
Malkin, C., 56
Manipulative play, 1, 5, 14; exploratory and nonexploratory activity in, 5–6; looking during, 11, 12. See also Exploratory activity; Exploratory play
Martinez, C., 47
Maslin-Cole, C. A., 32
Matas, L., 61

Matejcek, Z., 49
Melstein-Damast, A., 17
Mental abilities, and indexes of play, 22–23
Mentally retarded children, play of, 34–35
Menzel, E., 44
Miller, C., 56
Mitchell, D. W., 10, 11
Morbidity, and variability in play, 46–47
Morgan, G. A., 32
Most, R. K., 17, 18, 30, 44, 56, 60
Mothers: Japanese versus American, 60; and toddlers' level of play, 21. See also Caregivers
Motti, F., 34
Mundy, P., 29, 34, 35, 36

Nakamura, C., 49
Neimark, E., 67
Nelson, K., 17, 49
Neumann, C., 29, 33, 60, 62
Nicolich, L. M., 56, 68
Nonexploratory activity, 6–7
Nonsymbolic play, 26; and caregiver, 58–60; levels of, 20–21; and play in Kenya, 33
Nutrition, and play, 33, 47–49

O'Connell, B., 17, 23, 57, 58, 59, 62
O'Connor, N., 35
O'Donnell, K., 17, 23, 56, 62
O'Leary, K., 56
O'Reilly, A. W., 3, 55, 66
Ottinger, D. R., 35

Parke, R., 61
Parmelee, A. H., 10
Parrinello, R., 49
Pêcheux, M.-G., 11
Pedersen, F., 45
Perner, J., 39, 76
Perry, B. W., 34, 60
Piaget, J., 17, 43, 68, 70, 72, 74, 75
Pine, F., 68, 71
Play, 1; and caregivers, 55–62; constructive, 26; correlates of, 2, 32–33, 44–50; developmental progression in, 30–31; exploratory, 1; functional, 46; nonsymbolic, 20–21, 26, 33, 58–60; pretend, 2, 29–30; relational, 46; rep-

Play (*continued*)
  resentational, 71–77; social, 46; variability of, 43–44, 50–51. *See also* Correlates of play; Indexes of play; Manipulative play; Symbolic play
Play observations, 29–30, 38–39; of children with developmental disabilities, 34–38; and development, 30–31; of high-risk infants, 31–33
Pollitt, E., 46, 47
Posner, M. I., 13
Power, T. G., 26, 45, 61
Premack, D., 67
Pretend play, 2, 29–30. *See also* Manipulative play; Play observations

Qualitative measures, 18, 24–25. *See also* Level of sophistication
Quantitative measures, 18, 25. *See also* Duration of attention
Quinn, J., 49

Radke-Yarrow, M., 47
Ramsey, D. S., 56, 62
Relational play, 46
Representational ability, 23
Representational competence, 38; with autism, 35; with Down syndrome, 34; with mental retardation, 34–35; of pre-term infants, 32
Representational play, 71–72, 77; levels of, 72–75
Rheingold, H., 44
Riquet, C. B., 35
Rogers, C., 44
Rogoff, B., 56, 61
Rothbart, M. K., 9, 10, 13
Rothbart Infant Behavior Questionnaire, 9
Rubenstein, J., 45
Rubin, K., 17, 44, 49, 50
Ruff, H. A., 1, 5, 6, 7, 8, 11, 12, 13, 16, 26, 32, 49, 56, 67, 69
Ruskin, E., 34

Sachs, J., 56, 57, 61, 62
Sackett, G., 44
Saltarelli, L. M., 1, 5, 6, 7, 8, 13, 16, 26
Sartre, J.-P., 68, 69, 70
Schachtel, E. G., 8, 14, 68, 70, 75
Schmidt, M., 32, 44

Schwartzman, H., 43
Sena, R., 2, 21, 29, 42, 62
Sensorimotor exploration, 70–71
Shaheen, F., 43
Sherman, T., 35, 36
Shmukler, D., 45
Shore, C., 17, 18, 57, 62
Shotwell, J., 49, 50
Sigman, M. D., 2, 10, 19, 21, 26, 29, 31, 32, 33, 34, 35, 36, 39, 42, 46, 47, 56, 59, 60, 62
Slade, A., 44, 45, 57, 58, 61, 74
Snyder, L., 21
Social play, 46
Sophistication, 18. *See also* Level of sophistication
Spangler, G., 45, 61
Spenser, P. E., 60
Sroufe, L. A., 61
Sroufe, R. A., 34
Stern, D., 68
Stewart, P., 45, 60
Symbolic play, 26, 46; and caregiver, 58–60; levels of, 20–21; and nutrition, 47–48; and representational play, 75–76

Tal, J., 17, 23, 56, 62
Tamis-LeMonda, C. S., 1, 11, 17, 20, 22, 23, 24, 28, 30, 37, 56, 57, 58, 59, 60, 62
Tanaka, J., 17
Taylor, N. D., 35
Teti, D., 44
Thelen, E., 61, 75
Theory of mind, 76–77
Tilton, J. R., 35
Tingley, E. C., 60
Tomlinson-Keasey, C., 44

Udwin, O., 45
Unger, O., 59
Ungerer, J. A., 26, 29, 32, 33, 35, 36, 46, 56, 62
United States, symbolic play in, 60
Užgiris, I. C., 6, 68

Van Gulick, R., 71, 77, 78
Vandenberg, B., 17, 44, 49, 50
Vaughn, B. E., 30
Vibbert, M., 17, 18, 23, 50, 56, 60, 62
Vietze, P. M., 34
Vygotsky, L. S., 58, 71, 76

Wachs, T. D., 2, 21, 32, 43, 44, 45, 47, 48, 49, 53, 56, 62
Weiner, B., 35
Weisler, A., 43
Weiss, B., 34
Werner, H., 56, 67, 68, 69, 75
Wertsch, J. V., 58
West, M. J., 55
Wing, L., 35
Wolf, D., 49, 50
Wooding, C., 55, 56, 58, 59, 74

Woodruff, G., 67
Wright, B., 17

Yarrow, L., 44, 45
Yeates, S. R., 35
Yirmiya, N., 35
Yoder, P. J., 62
Yunis, F., 43

Zamor, M., 17
Zelazo, P. R., 56
Zukow, P. G., 58

Ordering Information

New Directions for Child Development is a series of paperback books that presents the latest research findings on all aspects of children's psychological development, including their cognitive, social, moral, and emotional growth. Books in the series are published quarterly in fall, winter, spring, and summer and are available for purchase by subscription as well as by single copy.

Subscriptions for 1993 cost $52.00 for individuals (a savings of 20 percent over single-copy prices) and $70.00 for institutions, agencies, and libraries. Please do not send institutional checks for personal subscriptions. Standing orders are accepted.

Single copies cost $17.95 when payment accompanies order. (California, New Jersey, New York, and Washington, D.C., residents please include appropriate sales tax.) Billed orders will be charged postage and handling.

Discounts for quantity orders are available. Please write to the address below for information.

All orders must include either the name of an individual or an official purchase order number. Please submit your order as follows:
  Subscriptions: specify series and year subscription is to begin
  Single copies: include individual title code (such as CD1)

Mail all orders to:
  Jossey-Bass Publishers
  350 Sansome Street
  San Francisco, California 94104

OTHER TITLES AVAILABLE IN THE
NEW DIRECTIONS FOR CHILD DEVELOPMENT SERIES
William Damon, Editor-in-Chief

CD58 Interpretive Approaches to Children's Socialization, *William A. Corsaro,*
Peggy J. Miller
CD57 Beyond the Parent: The Role of Other Adults in Children's Lives
Robert C. Pianta
CD56 The Development of Political Understanding: A New Perspective,
Helen Haste, Judith Torney-Purta
CD55 Emotion and Its Regulation in Early Development, *Nancy Eisenberg,*
Richard A. Fabes
CD54 Narrative and Storytelling: Implications for Understanding Moral
Development, *Mark B. Tappan, Martin J. Packer*
CD53 Academic Instruction in Early Childhood: Challenge or Pressure?
Leslie Rescorla, Marion C. Hyson, Kathy Hirsh-Pasek
CD52 Religious Development in Childhood and Adolescence, *Fritz K. Oser,*
W. George Scarlett
CD51 Shared Views in the Family During Adolescence, *Roberta L. Paikoff*
CD50 Adolescents in the AIDS Epidemic, *William Gardner, Susan G. Millstein,*
Brian L. Wilcox
CD49 Child Care and Maternal Employment: A Social Ecology Approach,
Kathleen McCartney
CD48 Children's Perspectives on the Family, *Inge Bretherton, Malcolm W. Watson*
CD47 The Legacy of Lawrence Kohlberg, *Dawn Schrader*
CD46 Economic Stress: Effects on Family Life and Child Development,
Vonnie C. McLoyd, Constance Flanagan
CD45 Infant Stress and Coping, Michael Lewis, *John Worobey*
CD44 Empathy and Related Emotional Responses, *Nancy Eisenberg*
CD42 Black Children and Poverty: A Developmental Perspective, *Diana T. Slaughter*
CD40 Parental Behavior in Diverse Societies, *Robert A. LeVine,*
Patrice M. Miller, Mary Maxwell West
CD39 Developmental Psychopathology and Its Treatment, *Ellen D. Nannis,*
Philip A. Cowan
CD37 Adolescent Social Behavior and Health, *Charles E. Irwin, Jr.*
CD36 Symbolic Development in Atypical Children, *Dante Cicchetti, Marjorie Beeghly*
CD35 How Children and Adolescents View the World of Work, *John H. Lewko*
CD31 Temperament and Social Interaction in Infants and Children,
Jacqueline V. Lerner, Richard M. Lerner
CD24 Children in Families Under Stress, *Anna-Beth Doyle, Dolores Gold,*
Debbie S. Moscowitz
CD22 Adolescent Development in the Family, *Harold D. Grotevant, Catherine R. Cooper*
CD19 Children and Divorce, *Lawrence A. Kurdek*